Minutes to Midnight

Minutes to Midnight

History and the Anthropocene Era from 1763

Paul Dukes

ANTHEM PRESS
LONDON · NEW YORK · DELHI

Anthem Press
An imprint of Wimbledon Publishing Company
www.anthempress.com

This edition first published in UK and USA 2011
by ANTHEM PRESS
75-76 Blackfriars Road, London SE1 8HA, UK
or PO Box 9779, London SW19 7ZG, UK
and
244 Madison Ave. #116, New York, NY 10016, USA

British Library Cataloguing in Publication Data
A catalogue record for this book is available from the British Library.

Library of Congress Cataloging-in-Publication Data

Dukes, Paul, 1934-
Minutes to midnight : history and the Anthropocene era from 1763 / Paul Dukes.
p. cm. – (Anthem world history)
Includes bibliographical references and index.
ISBN 978-0-85728-779-3 (hardcover) – ISBN 978-0-85728-780-9 (papercover)

This title is also available as an eBook.

To Samuel, Francesca, Ike and their generation

CONTENTS

PREFACE

In 1947, the Doomsday Clock was created by a group of atomic scientists to symbolise the perils facing humanity from nuclear weapons. Sixty years on, in 2007, after many readjustments, it was set at five minutes before the final bell. The reasons given by the scientists included – for the first time – new developments in the life sciences and nanotechnology, and the threat of climate change (*Bulletin of the Atomic Scientists*, 17 January 2007, accessed online 3 March 2011). In 2010, with some evidence of movement towards arms and climate control, the Clock was taken back to six minutes to midnight. The scientists declared: 'For the first time in decades we have an opportunity to free ourselves from the terror of nuclear weapons and to slow drastic changes to our shared global environment.' They encouraged 'scientists to continue their engagement with these issues and make their analysis widely known', and were confident enough to assert: 'We are poised to bend the arc of history' (*Bulletin of the Atomic Scientists*, 14 January 2010, accessed online 3 March 2011). It is highly unlikely that the atomic scientists would include historians among those 'poised to bend the arc of history', and even less likely that most historians would want to be included. However, this book takes the contrary view, arguing for the necessity of history as a science in a pandisciplinary response to the ongoing crisis.

It begins with the onset of the Anthropocene Era – the recent geological phase during which human activities have had a global impact upon the planet. The era began in the latter part of the eighteenth century, when available data indicates the beginning of a growth in the atmospheric concentrations of several greenhouse gases. This period includes James Watt's fundamental improvement of the steam engine, the event central to the Industrial Revolution that transformed the face of the world and began to pollute it.

Watt's achievement is the point of departure for this book, which seeks to describe some significant aspects of the coincidence of geological time with historical time. It has three major interlocking aims: 1) to note major advances in the natural sciences and their applications; 2) to set out an analytical narrative of the Anthropocene Era; 3) to pay particular attention to the development of history as an academic discipline in association with other humanities, the social and natural sciences, and to illustrate its response to the changing circumstances of successive periods.

1) To be clear from the beginning, an author who finds even the workings of the steam engine difficult to grasp should not attempt to do more than recognise the most significant scientific and technical innovations from Watt's onwards. Therefore, I intend to discuss what has happened more broadly, and what has been written about it, in a manner begun by Watt's contemporaries, Adam Smith and Adam Ferguson.

2) I believe that there is one fundamental narrative concerning the Anthropocene Era, although I concede that there can be discussion about its direction from the eighteenth century onwards. Up to 1945 I concentrate on Europe and the USA, where the Industrial Revolution most clearly unfolded, thus enabling these powers to dominate other continents. The focus of the book then widens, as in the twentieth century the A-bomb and then the H-bomb threatened to bring the human story to an end during the worldwide processes of the cold war and decolonisation. Development of atomic power for peaceful purposes was deemed a necessity by some experts as the additional problem of climate change emerged and the exhaustion of fossil fuels approached. By the late 1960s, the Chinese detonation of an H-bomb demonstrated that the world dominance of Europe and the USA was coming to an end, and ecological problems intensified. Clearly, the fundamental narrative does not indicate positive progress exclusively, and moreover it is relentless in its approach towards a palpable and abrupt conclusion.

3) I shall spell out how historians and other investigators have tackled the problem of interpretation, using as a yardstick the comprehensive arguments concerning global stadial development put forward by Smith and Ferguson in the eighteenth century. I shall argue that, after developing these arguments in the nineteenth century, historians and colleagues in other disciplines tended to ignore or distort them in the

twentieth. From the late twentieth century onwards, however, with the end of the cold war, opportunities have opened for the full resumption of the Enlightenment agenda. Indeed, I shall argue that, in view of the still menacing setting of the Doomsday Clock at six minutes to midnight, the resumption of rational, global and evolutionary analysis, taking full cognisance of the differences between the late eighteenth century and the early twenty-first century, has become a necessity for historians uniquely qualified to assess the significance for humankind of the passage of time. The necessity will remain even if the Clock moves back more minutes from the fateful hour, since the complexities of the era will still be with us. To put the point simply, anthropocentric history must increasingly be replaced by an anthropocenic approach – a change of just two letters, but one that offers a world of difference – which would place the study of the past together with the humane, social and natural sciences in a pandisciplinary amalgam. To justify this assertion is the ultimate purpose of the book as a whole.

Of course, I accept full responsibility for *Minutes to Midnight*. But it is not all my own work, and I have relied heavily on the books and articles cited in the endnotes. In addition, I thank Routledge and Palgrave Macmillan respectively for permission to include passages from *World Order in History* (1996) and *Paths to a New Europe* (2004). Moreover, I could not have completed the book without the generous help of others. I acknowledge with deep gratitude the incisive comments made by my wife Cathryn, a fellow historian with a background in science. Many thanks also to Michael Dey, Murray Frame, Graeme P. Herd, Jean Houbert and Ian Thatcher for their thorough reading and constructive suggestions. I am extremely grateful to Marshall Poe, who first convinced me of the advantages of electronic publication and gave essential advice on how to approach it, and who also introduced me to Anthem Press, where Tej Sood, Janka Romero and Robert Reddick have been especially supportive. At the University of Aberdeen, as ever, I have benefitted from the counsel and encouragement of colleagues old and new in the History and other departments. The secretarial support of Gillian Brown and Barbara McGillivray has been vital, as has the advice of associates of the computer help desk and Queen Mother Library. The book is dedicated to my grandchildren, with hopes that the hands of the Doomsday Clock will move far from midnight during their lifetime. It was my first meeting with Samuel early in 2008 that inspired me to put aside other projects to embark on this one that seemed to have more urgency, and the arrival of Francesca and Ike in mid-2010 that has helped me to complete it.

Acknowledging again that the errors and misunderstandings in this book are all mine, I should nevertheless like to ask critical readers, what do *you* think should be the role of the study of history at the present stage of the Anthropocene Era?

Paul Dukes
King's College, Old Aberdeen
March 2011

Chapter 1

INTRODUCTION:
TIMES AND APPROACHES

The tiny spheroid that we call home hurtles through space as if there were no tomorrow. A thin surface crust covers a molten mass of which we know comparatively little. Surrounding the earth is a cocoon of atmosphere, which we understand rather better.

Recently we have learned that there may indeed be no tomorrow, since human-made changes are making an impact on the world's ecosystems that could bring to an end life as we have known it. This, in addition to the continuing possibility of a suicidal nuclear war, and the added threat of mass destruction posed by new technologies.

Earlier geological ages either predated or proceeded without significant interference from our ancestors. Respectful of nature in their own way, 'primitive' human beings often worshipped the sun and moon, making sacrifices to appease them or the gods of nature. The emergence of the great religions brought about change in this relationship, introducing the idea that man could, or even should, dominate nature. Confidence was even greater among some materialists. For example, the Soviet historian M. N. Pokrovsky declared in 1931: 'It is easy to foresee that in future, when science and technique have attained to a perfection which we are as yet unable to visualise, nature will become soft wax in his [man's] hands which he will be able to cast into whatever form he chooses.'[1] Sixty years later, by the time of the collapse of the Soviet Union, such confidence was all too obviously misplaced.

Nearly a century-and-a-half earlier, in 1785, James Hutton read papers to the Royal Society of Edinburgh arguing that the earth had been in existence for much longer than the 6,000 years that appeared to be allowed by Bible, with 'no vestige of a beginning – no prospect of an end'.[2] The need for a label for the postglacial geological epoch of the past 10,000 to 12,000 years was probably suggested by Sir Charles Lyell in 1833: 'holocene', meaning 'recent whole', gradually gained acceptance throughout Europe and beyond, and was accepted by the International Geological Congress in Bologna in 1885. Charles Darwin took Lyell's *Principles of Geology* (1830–33) with him on the voyage of the Beagle as he began to formulate the ideas that would find their classic formulation in *The Origin of Species*, first published in 1859.

A book entitled *The Biosphere* was produced in 1926 by Vladimir Vernadsky, which combined Darwinism more closely with ecology in its suggestions that the earth's surface was the product of biological activity, and that since the eighteenth century human beings had increased greatly the quantity of biogenic gases. Along with others, Vernadsky suggested that the human race would transform the biosphere into the 'noosphere' – the sphere of the mind – while a new world-view – cosmism – would involve the reduction of chaos on earth and in space through united human effort.[3]

The use of the atomic bomb in 1945 created an immediate danger. In 1947, the Doomsday Clock was created by a group of elite scientists to symbolise the perils facing humanity from nuclear weapons, with midnight representing 'catastrophic destruction'.[4] In 1953, it reached a mere two minutes from the fatal hour after the USA and USSR had both detonated hydrogen bombs. The danger was even greater at the time of the Cuban Missile Crisis in 1962. In 1991, with the fall of the USSR, the clock reached its furthest point from doom – seventeen minutes to midnight. Then, in 2002, after 9/11, it was advanced ten minutes – then showing seven minutes to midnight. Sixty years after its first appearance, in 2007, it moved forward again – to five minutes before the final bell would toll for us all. The reasons given by the clock-setting scientists were growing anxieties concerning world terrorism, the nuclear ambitions of Iran and North Korea and – for the first time – 'new developments in the life sciences and nanotechnology that could inflict irrevocable harm', as well as the threat of global warming. 'The dangers posed by climate change are nearly as dire as those posed by nuclear weapons', the scientists stated, adding: 'The effects may be less dramatic in the short term than the destruction that could be wrought by nuclear explosions, but over the next three to four decades climate change could cause irremediable harm to the habitats upon which human societies depend for survival.' This was in addition to the threat posed by some thousands of nuclear weapons in the USA and Russia, as well as the further considerable number possessed by other powers, especially China. 'Not since the first atomic bombs were dropped on Hiroshima and Nagasaki has the world faced such perilous choices',[5] the scientists declared. These observations were made by the Board of Directors of the Bulletin of the Atomic Scientists in consultation with its board of sponsors, which included no fewer than 18 Nobel laureates. In 2010, the Board pushed the clock back from five to six minutes before midnight, having found 'signs of a growing political will to tackle the two gravest threats to civilization – the terror of nuclear weapons and runaway climate change.' It called for further progress from scientists and others, asserting: 'We are poised to bend the arc of history'.[6]

In the year 2000, the concept of an Anthropocene Era was put forward by the Nobel laureate Paul J. Crutzen and his colleague Eugene F. Stoermer, amplifying the earlier suggestion of Vladimir Vernadsky. But when did this era begin? To quote these two scientists:

> To assign a more specific date to the onset of the 'anthropocene' seems somewhat arbitrary, but we propose the latter part of the eighteenth century, although we are aware that alternative proposals can be made (some may even want to include the entire holocene). However, we choose this date because, during the past two centuries, the global effects of human activities have become clearly noticeable. This is the period when data retrieved from glacial ice cores show the beginning of a growth in the atmospheric concentrations of several 'greenhouse gases', in particular CO_2 and CH_4. Such a starting date also coincides with James Watt's invention of the steam engine in 1784. About at that time, biotic assemblages in most lakes began to show large deleterious changes.[7]

Of course, to choose any single date in a discussion of hundreds of years of change in the exploitation of the earth is indeed arbitrary. But it would be arrogant and dangerous in the extreme at this point or any later point in this book for a historian to make any observations about natural science. I shall therefore confine myself to reporting the remarks of others qualified to make them on this subject. However, the arbitrary nature of the choice of a single date applies to history as much as science. Here, and for reasons I shall elaborate in particular in chapter two, I choose the year 1763.

Before 1763, more generally, there had been many millions of years of geology and several thousands of years of history. Even if we confine ourselves to the emergence of the Western civilisation that first produced atomic weapons and industrial pollution, the task of describing the move from the primitive to the more advanced stages of development via the ancient, medieval and early modern periods is impossibly daunting. So let us just note simply that there is a case for maintaining that modern Europe began to arise in the seventeenth century with the formation of states, the growth of capitalism and the beginnings of a secular culture (including a scientific revolution). The Anthropocene Era itself takes us through three main phases of human history: the pre-industrial before c. 1850; the industrial from c.1850 to c.1970; and the post-industrial from c.1970.[8]

A few more preliminary points. First, while science is without doubt history, history is not necessarily science. Of course, the manner in which various sciences handle history's major characteristic, the passage of time, varies enormously over the centuries. Geology, accustomed to deal in millions of years or more, has now turned some of its focus onto a period of about two hundred years, as we have just seen. To remind ourselves of another metaphorical clock, if the world's existence is represented as a day, human beings arrive in the final seconds. To help us further to think flexibly about time, let us turn to the example of physics: today's researchers may deal in billions of years or nanoseconds.

To continue with the same example, the author of a reputable textbook could assert as late as 1902: 'Physics has been on sure ground since the publication of Newton's *Principia* (1687).'[9] In fact, a paradigm change in physics was occurring at the beginning of the twentieth century, fulfilling the basic criterion of Thomas S. Kuhn: 'To be accepted as a paradigm, a theory must seem better than its competitors, but it need not, and in fact never does, explain all the facts with which it can be confronted.'[10] In a comparable manner, the Kuhnian definition may be applied to the study of history at the beginning of the twentieth century. Roundabout that time, a great change was widely recommended for the discipline, breaking the nation-centred conventions that had been normal throughout the nineteenth century, and developing some of the universal principles first established by colleagues of James Watt in the Scottish Enlightenment and comparatively neglected since.

The First World War dealt a serious blow to ideas of universal history, elevating patriotic distortion to great heights. Between the wars, there was a continuance of nationalistic history, sometimes of an extreme kind, especially in Nazi Germany and Fascist Italy. In Soviet Russia, there was an energetic attempt to develop the universalist approach on a Marxist basis before the dead hand of Stalinism crushed it. Then, the Second World War took history to a super-patriotic level everywhere. Immediately afterwards, unfortunately, the implications of the arrival of the atomic bomb for the subject were not immediately realised. In many ways, study continued with a national focus, with a celebration of the histories of the victors and condemnation of the histories of the losers. Nevertheless, there were some signs of a wider framework, as we shall see in the example of the concept of 'total history' advocated in France by Fernand Braudel, who also talked of three orders of time represented by the concepts 'event', 'conjuncture' and 'structure'.[11] While the cold war and decolonisation made for deep divisions in the world community as well as threatening to bring it to an end, the ensuing process of globalisation encouraged historians and others to look further outwards. This widening of focus was suggested further by organisations such as the Club of Rome and the Brandt Commission, and by individuals such as Rachel Carson and James Lovelock giving serious consideration to the growing ecological world crisis.

By the beginning of the twenty-first century, however, there was no clear sign of an approach to the study of history reflecting the message of the Doomsday Clock. As a contribution to the fulfilment of an urgent task, I shall attempt to note the most significant scientific and technical advances from James Watt's contribution onwards, while concentrating on the mainstream of human development and what has been written about it, in a manner that aspires to be 'scientific'. Arthur Herman writes of Watt's contemporaries, Scottish savants in the last quarter of the eighteenth century, that their dominant works shared two themes, 'history' and 'human nature', which they first linked together when they presented man as the product of history:

> Our most fundamental character as human beings, they argued, even our moral character, is constantly evolving and developing, shaped by a variety of forces over which we as individuals have little or no control. We are ultimately creatures of our environment: that was the great discovery that the 'Scottish school', as it came to be known, brought to the modern world.

Moreover, Herman points out, the Scottish writers 'also insisted that these changes are not arbitrary or chaotic. They rest on certain fundamental principles and discernible patterns. The study of man is ultimately a *scientific* study.'[12]

In his otherwise excellent book *Why History Matters* (2008), John Tosh complains that 'intimations of disaster held out first by nuclear weapons and now by global warming' join ideas of 'progress without a hinterland in the past', to 'encourage belief in a world which is fashioned anew, to all practical purposes without a history'.[13] But he makes little or no attempt to suggest that the disaster threatening humankind does indeed have a history, beginning in the West in Europe and the USA, the first homes of industrial revolution, and then enveloping the whole world.

Thus, there is a broad gap in urgent need of filling, however many and great the further difficulties along the way. One of these is the reluctance to consider history a science, especially in the English-speaking world where linguistic convention has accompanied deep-set tradition. The collapse of Soviet Marxism-Leninism is deemed to have driven the last nail into the coffin of scientific history. Moreover, indeed, history can probably never be an exact science, since it is subject to so many accidents, variables and otherwise unforeseen circumstances. However, volcanoes present similar difficulties, yet nobody would deny that volcanology is a science. Of course, close analogy is impossible, especially since human behaviour is more unpredictable than that of inanimate, however volatile matter. A central problem here is the role of the individual. Let us take the example of scientists, on which John Gribbin has written:

> If Newton had never lived, scientific progress might have been held back by a few decades. Edmond Halley or Robert Hooke might well have come up with the famous inverse square law of gravity. Gottfried Leibniz actually did invent calculus independently of Newton (and made a better job of it); and Christian Huygens's superior wave theory of light was held back by Newton's espousal of the rival particle theory.

Conceding nevertheless that Newton is something of a special case, Gribbin insists that scientific progress occurs step-by-step, and that it is 'the luck of the draw, or historical accident, whose name gets remembered as the discoverer of a new phenomenon'. Gribbin argues that, while to talk of individuals is to advance the narrative process, the development of technology is much more important than human genius, adding 'it is no surprise that the start of the scientific revolution "coincides" with the development of the telescope and the microscope'.[11] Later, James Watt's special achievement was that 'he was the first person to take a set of ideas from the cutting edge of then-current research in science and apply them to a major technical advance'. Consequently, 'in the second half of the eighteenth century, Watt's improvements to the steam engine were very high-tech indeed; and it was the whole style of Watt's approach that pointed the way for the development of technology in the nineteenth and twentieth centuries.' Moreover, 'once the Industrial Revolution got under way, it gave a huge boost to science.'[15]

What about the individual in 'mainstream' history? We cannot easily say that, if Napoleon had not lived, history's 'progress might have been held back by a few decades.' People like him have to seize the moment, and those who hesitate are often lost. At the same time, we would have to accept for historical actors what Gribbin says about scientists – that the development of technology is much more important than human genius. Thus, all prominent men and women in the Anthropocene Era have operated under the influence of the ongoing Industrial Revolution and scientific advance. For example, Harry S. Truman has often been considered one of the greatest American presidents of the twentieth century. He would not have achieved this distinction without the A-bomb.

This is not to reduce the individual to a cipher. One of the best assessments remains that of Plekhanov:

A great man is great not because his personal qualities give individual features to great historical events, but because he possesses qualities which make him most capable of serving the great social needs of his time, needs which arose as a result of general and particular causes. Carlyle, in his well-known book on heroes and hero-worship, calls great men *beginners*. This is a very apt description. A great man is precisely a beginner because he sees *further* than others, and desires things *more strongly* than others. He solves the scientific problems brought up by the preceding process of intellectual development of society; he points to the new social needs created by the preceding development of social relationships; he takes the initiative in satisfying these needs. He is a hero. But he is not a hero in the sense that he can stop, or change, the natural course of things, but in the sense that his activities are the conscious and free expression of the inevitable and unconscious course. Herein lies all his significance; herein lies his whole power. But this significance is colossal, and the power is terrible.[16]

What Plekhanov wrote in 1898 was echoed by Braudel in 1965; paradoxically he observed that 'the true man of action is he who can measure most nearly the constraints upon him, who chooses to remain within them and even to take advantage of the weight of the inevitable, exerting his own pressure in the same direction'. Braudel added that he was always inclined to see the individual 'imprisoned within a destiny in which he himself has little hand, fixed in a landscape in which the infinite perspectives of the long term stretch into the distance both behind him and before'.[17] Here is an unwitting echo of James Hutton nearly two centuries before: 'no vestige of a beginning – no prospect of an end'. Nearly fifty years on, however, the future is less certain, and the role of the individual even more restricted as the anthropocenic increasingly replaces the anthropocentric.

Though individuals are restricted in their freedom of movement throughout history, to talk of them certainly helps the narrative along. And history is nothing without narrative, the description of human society's movement through time. But where does the narrative end? The convention is that it has no end, and to suggest otherwise is to invite the charge of a distorting teleology. Teleology has two definitions: in theology, the doctrine of design and purpose in the material world; in philosophy, the explanation of phenomena by the purpose they serve. Since they involve supernatural phenomena, theological considerations cannot be included in secular historical discussion, particularly if we apply to it the words of the progenitor of Christianity as reported by St Matthew: 'Render therefore unto Caesar the things which are Caesar's; and unto God the things that are God's' (Matthew 22:21). Caesar acts, God judges. The empire that Caesar helped to create attempted to impose its so-called *Pax Romana* upon as much of the world as possible, and to use this concept as an important part of its self-justification, confidently explaining phenomena by the purpose they served – might was right.[18] A series of successors have acted in a similar manner, most of them making the additional claim of God's support and sanction.

Of course, Holy Writ is open to interpretation, and there has been no shortage of theologians acting as spokesmen for empire. Ultimately, however, as indicated by imperial decline and fall, Ecclesiastes would appear to have hit the nail on the head in the assertion that 'all is vanity' (Ecclesiastes 1:2). Human history might well come to an end and God make his final judgement. From a materialistic point of view, a colleague who will remain anonymous has written that 'the best thing that could happen to the planet is the disappearance of human beings'.

Generally speaking, Western historians speak against teleology in times of tranquillity, but favour it in times of turmoil. A famous British example in this respect is Herbert Butterfield, who brought out a book in 1931 with the title *The Whig Interpretation of History*, criticising the tendency 'to emphasise certain principles of progress in the past and to produce a story which is the ratification if not the glorification of the present'.[19] In 1944, however, in *The Englishman and His History*, Butterfield wrote of 'the Englishman's alliance with his history' and of 'the marriage between the present and the past'.[20]

If Butterfield could overcome earlier reservations concerning the use of history during the Second World War, should we not follow his example when faced with the graver crisis of the extinction of humanity? Moreover, if the ship is sinking, all hands must be called to the pumps. That is to say, in putting forward the argument that the past might again be married to the present, we will not define the discipline of history narrowly, but rather make use of the work of a considerable range of authorities on aspects of human society's movement through time.

Let us be clear from the beginning. What is scientific history? Above all, it is rational, global and evolutionary. First, the victories of unthinking brute force in the past should not mean the present abandonment of the still, small voice of reason. Secondly, it must overcome individual, local, national, continental or ideological partiality, avoiding above all triumphalist celebration or humiliating self-abasement, condemnation or praise. Thirdly, passage through time must be handled with extreme care. For example, the Western post-industrial society of today, coexisting with Eastern industrialising society, differs radically from the pre-industrial society of more than two centuries ago.

In the next chapter on the Enlightenment and revolutions, we shall examine both the achievement of James Watt and the arguments of Adam Smith and Adam Ferguson concerning the stadial development

of human society from the primitive period through to the eighteenth
century. These arguments must not be treated as timeless axioms, but
as part of an evolving intellectual tradition, profoundly affected by the
incipient Industrial Revolution along with the American and French
revolutions.[21]

In the tradition of the Enlightenment, then, the book will sketch
the advancement of science, the narrative of history and the study of
the past during the most recent two-and-a-half centuries, each chapter
carrying the analysis a stage further towards the final exposition of the
case for pandisciplinarity.

Chapter 2

ENLIGHTENMENT AND
REVOLUTIONS, 1763–1815

As we have seen in the previous chapter, Crutzen and Stoermer concede that to assign a specific date to the onset of the Anthropocene Era seems 'somewhat arbitrary'. However, they suggest that the new era began in the latter part of the eighteenth century, because the initial creation of 'greenhouse gases' and 'biotic assemblages' occurred at the same time as James Watt's 'invention of the steam engine in 1784'.[1] Here, we might also appear arbitrary in our choice of the year 1763. However, this is not a random selection, for the following reasons.

Let us briefly recall the argument of our introduction: that evidence from the study of history and other humanities, as well as from the social and natural sciences, must be examined in any adequate analysis of the Anthropocene Era, and that it is the history on which we will concentrate. In 1763, a significant global conflict came to an end. It was marked by a victory of Great Britain over France, whose power was broken in Canada and India and reduced in Europe. The way was clear for Great Britain to become the workshop of the world via the Industrial Revolution. For example, K. N. Chaudhuri observes: 'The final stage in the dynamic movements in the Indian Ocean was reached in the second half of the eighteenth century when British military and naval power fused with European technological revolution to redraw the civilisational map of the Indian Ocean.'[2] At the same time, the road was opening up towards the political upheavals of the American and French revolutions.

James Watt and the First Industrial Revolution

In the same year as peace was restored, 1763, James Watt in Glasgow 'tried some experiments on the force of steam', to use his own words.

After intense study, he claimed that he had finally clarified the principles of his later achievements. In the winter of 1763–4, he repaired and modified a model of the widely-used Newcomen engine for a class at the College, as the university was then called. Watt was to assert that he began this work as 'a mere mechanician' but soon developed into a man of science. In 1774, he entered a partnership with Matthew Boulton in Birmingham, and in 1775, after some setbacks, the pair was granted an extended patent that lasted up to 1800. This has been called 'the most important event in the Industrial Revolution'.[3] Without it, the mechanical impetus for the transformation of the economy would have been delayed, not only in Britain but also throughout Europe, the USA and elsewhere. Having made a major contribution to the development of the concept of the 'horsepower', Watt was posthumously honoured by the British Association for the Advancement of Science in 1882 with the assignment of his name to the unit of power that we recall when we handle a light bulb, as the first stage of the Industrial Revolution gave way to the second.

James Watt would not have achieved immortality without the context evolving after 1763, nor without the help of friends. These included not only his business partner Matthew Boulton, but also many at Glasgow College, in the Lunar Society of Birmingham and elsewhere. Let us take three examples that illustrate Watt's wider significance and put it in context. First, James Hutton, the 'fossil philosopher' who agreed to travel in the company of that other amateur geologist, James Watt, on the way to Birmingham in 1774. Later, in 1785, James Hutton read papers to the Royal Society of Edinburgh arguing the case for uniformitarianism, the principle that the same processes were at work moulding the earth's surface continually, with 'no vestige of a beginning, no prospect of an end',[4] and for much longer than the 6,000 years or so allowed by the reading of the Bible then current. Second among Watt's acquaintances, John Robison, later professor at Edinburgh University, who attempted unsuccessfully to attract him to Russia in 1771 as 'Master Founder of Iron Ordinance'; movement was soon in the other direction as Russian apprentices and mechanics came to learn from Watt in England.[5] Third, William Small, from Marischal College Aberdeen and former tutor of Thomas Jefferson at William and Mary College in Virginia, who was of great help to Watt from their first meeting via Benjamin Franklin in 1765 to his death in 1775. Ben Marsden comments: 'Until 1775, Small kept the Scotsman flying, consoling him with a stream of encouraging letters as worries about his health drifted to despair of steam and its sickly mechanical progeny.' In 1786, perhaps partly in memory of Small, Jefferson and the American ambassador to Britain, John Adams, attempted to visit the Albion mill at Blackfriars, London. They were refused admittance 'due to England's laws protecting industrial secrets'.[6]

Adam Smith and Adam Ferguson: The Stages of Historical Development

Coincidentally, the year 1776 saw not only the American Declaration of Independence but also the publication of a highly significant product of the Scottish Enlightenment – *An Inquiry into the Nature and Causes of the Wealth of Nations*. Its author Adam Smith is widely hailed as the advocate of the unfettered market, and of its 'hidden hand' in particular. However, he himself wanted *The Wealth of Nations* to be considered as part of his philosophical, historical and economic work as a whole. In particular, this would include *The Theory of Moral Sentiments*, first published in London in 1759, and another book on the general principles of law and government that he never completed. For Smith, man was to be found not in isolation but in society, held together by the essential condition of sympathy. He suggested that: 'How selfish soever man may be supposed, there are evidently some principles in his nature which interest him in the fortunes of others, and render their happiness necessary to him, though he derives nothing from it except the pleasure of seeing it.'[7] Moreover, his actions were to be judged not only by his own conscience but also by some external agency.

As an active being, man would move through four stages of economic growth, which Smith described as 'hunting, pasturage, farming, and commerce'. He showed most interest in the last two and the relationship evolving between them with the division of labour and the increased necessity of exchange. While Smith viewed the state as exercising minimum restraint on the market mechanism, his thinking was governed by an acute consciousness of historical time, observing of particular conditions that 'the circumstances, which first gave occasion to them, and which could alone render them reasonable, are no more'.[8]

Certainly, some of the world was on the move. 'Since the discovery of America', Smith observed, 'the greater part of Europe has been much improved. England, Holland, France, and Germany; even Sweden, Denmark, and Russia, have all advanced considerably both in agriculture and in manufactures.'[9] So the commercial stage of human development was well under way. But Smith could say nothing about the industrial and post-industrial stages of development, ensuing well after his death – a point often forgotten by latter-disciples of Adam Smith, some of whom have shown scant acquaintance with the writings of the master. Indeed, the very title of his major work has been misunderstood: 'wealth' does not mean just riches but also comprises 'commonwealth', the general good.

Another misunderstood concept is the apparently impersonal agency of the 'invisible hand', which has been cited on countless occasions although mentioned only once in *The Wealth of Nations*. Referring to the pursuit of self-interest by the individual, Smith wrote that 'he is in this, as in many other cases, led by an invisible hand to promote an end which was no part of his intention.'[10] However, this observation should not be used to assist in the assertion of impersonal forces. As Michael Dey points out, Smith's contemporary Adam Ferguson put the point more clearly in *An Essay on the History of Civil Society* (1767). The passage deserves quotation at length:

> Every step and every movement of the multitude, even in what are termed enlightened ages, are made with equal blindness to the future; and nations stumble upon [political] establishments, which are indeed the result of human action, but not the execution of any human design. If Cromwell said, That a man never mounts higher, than when he knows not whither he is going; it may with more reason be affirmed of communities, that they admit of the greatest revolutions where no change is intended, and that the most refined politicians do not always know whither they are leading the state by their projects.[11]

As Dey suggests, 'This conception of the invisible hand we can liken to the idea of gravity found in eighteenth century thought. The natural philosophers could not say what gravity was, but they could posit its existence and relate the external phenomena of the universe to this organisational principle.'[12]

Ferguson's source on this matter, the Cardinal de Retz, for his part, uses both medicine and mechanics among other metaphors in a subtle analysis of human behaviour that merits further attention. Retz's *Mémoires* deserve scrutiny for two reasons: in their own right; and as a reminder that Smith and Ferguson both make use of past writers in their own work, such as Newton and Montesquieu for example, as well as the ancient classics. Thus, they more clearly take their place in an evolving tradition, and point the way to future writers. On the turbulent events of the Frondes in France in 1649–50, Retz writes that 'certainly, there was not one of all those giving their opinion...who had the least idea not only of what would come of them, but of what could come of them'. One of the main reasons for this was the power of the masses as represented in their collective imagination. Of this, Retz observes, 'one could truly say that in distinction to all other kinds of power, they are capable when they came to a certain point of all that they believe they are capable.'[13]

In general, Derek A. Watts comments, 'Retz attempts to analyse and predict the behaviour of collectivities in the same manner as he studies the psychology of individuals. He shows how crowds and assemblies can be controlled and exploited by faction leaders who have acquired the necessary "science"'. However, Watts continues, Retz also reveals that 'mass psychology cannot always be understood simply as a sum total, a resultant of so many individual impulses. There are phenomena peculiar to the mob, in which human beings are liable to behave in a quite unpredictable manner.'[14] Here, then, is an anticipation of the 'invisible hand', underlining that it does not comprise impersonal forces.

Yet another misunderstood concept advanced by Adam Smith is that of the 'impartial spectator'. As Dey points out, this is not 'some wholly detached, a-historical, a-social phenomenon' but one 'constrained within...and formed by actual social development'.[15] The socially interactive process was illustrated by Smith's observation made in the late 1750s: 'If we saw ourselves in the light in which others see us, or in which they would see us if they knew all, a reformation would be generally unavoidable.'[16]

In this respect, the reservations should be noted concerning the direction being taken by stadial progression in the eighteenth century, particularly those of Ferguson Here is the man often credited for minting the much-used term 'civil society' but also warning about dangers inherent in its formation: the last two parts of his book consist 'Of the Decline of Nations' and 'Of Corruption and Political Slavery'.

To be sure, these were a warning, not a prediction. The division of labour and the growing complexity of society as a whole, Ferguson considered, brought new dangers as well as fresh possibilities. For example, he wrote, 'any immoderate increase of private expence [sic] is a prelude to national weakness: government, even while each of its subjects consumes a princely estate, may be straitened in point of revenue, and the paradox be explained by example, That the public is poor, while its members are rich.' Moreover, while human institutions were 'likely to have their end as well as their beginning', the length of their duration was not fixed, and 'no nation ever suffered internal decay but from the vice of its members'.[17] Even at the commercial stage of human development, then, dangers were already apparent that would emerge more clearly in the industrial and post-industrial stages. Of course, we must be careful to avoid the temptation to apply Ferguson's ideas of 'civil society' too literally to these later stages.[18]

Let us make clear the British situation at the commercial stage. As Smith put it: 'The inhabitants of many different parts of Great Britain have not capital sufficient to improve and cultivate all their lands. The wool of the southern counties of Scotland is, a great part of it, after a long land carriage through very bad roads, manufactured in Yorkshire, for want of capital to manufacture it at home.'[19]

This was the setting in which James Watt travelled south with James Hutton en route for Birmingham. In general, we need to recognise, Smith gave primacy among economic pursuits to agriculture, concluding: 'The ordinary revolutions of war and government easily dry up the sources of that wealth which arises from commerce only. That which arises from the more solid improvements of agriculture is much more durable…' Moreover, he noted: 'It has been the principal cause of the rapid progress of our American colonies towards wealth and greatness, that almost their whole capitals have hitherto been employed in agriculture.'[20] Smith, then, was an advocate as well as an analyst of the pre-industrial mode of life.

Let us recall that his famous example of the advantages of the assembly line, used for pin-making, included a mechanical operation without benefit of a steam engine. This classic description of the division of labour, enabling the production by ten men of more than 48,000 pins a day, as opposed to a single man not necessarily producing one of them, mentions nothing more than the simplest of machinery. To be sure, the steam engine is indeed mentioned in *The Wealth of*

Nations, but only in the shape of the earliest version known as the 'fire-engine', improved by a boy employed to open and shut alternately the communication between the boiler and the cylinder. Smith observes: 'It was a real philosopher [scientist] only who could invent the fire-engine, and first form the idea of producing so great an effect by a power of nature which had never before been thought of.' Smith continues: 'Many inferior artists, employed in the fabric of this wonderful machine, may afterwards discover more happy methods of applying that power than those first made use of by its illustrious inventer [sic].' But he makes no specific mention of James Watt and his improvements.[21]

The American and French Revolutions

In 1776, the year of the publication of *The Wealth of Nations*, the American colonies declared their independence. One of the principal architects of this revolutionary move, Thomas Jefferson, wrote to James Watt's friend and his own mentor William Small in 1775, lamenting that the shooting of hundreds of 'brethren in Boston' by 'the king's troops' had 'cut off our last hopes of reconciliation, and a phrenzy of revenge seems to have seized all ranks of people.' Could it be believed, asked Jefferson, that 'a grateful people will suffer those to be consigned to execution whose sole crime has been the developing and asserting their rights?'[22]

The Declaration of Independence of 1776, as it became known, consisted mainly of an itemised condemnation of the 'absolute Despotism' of George III. Its composition was evidently imbued with the spirit of the Enlightenment as well as other influences. Especially noteworthy is the substitution of 'the pursuit of Happiness' for property, which had more normally been juxtaposed with life and liberty since the Glorious Revolution of 1689 in England, Scotland and Ireland. Much later, in 1810, Jefferson wrote: 'To lose our country by a scrupulous adherence to written law, would be to lose the law itself, with life, liberty, property and all those who are enjoying them with us.' In the case of the American Revolution and other crises, 'the unwritten laws of necessity, of self-preservation, and of the public safety, control the written laws of *meum* and *tuum*…'[23] Thus, 'the pursuit of Happiness' which would include security was substituted for property in the Declaration of Independence, and an early assertion of human rights given its distinctive character.

Another point must be given emphasis. To the end of his life, like Adam Smith, Jefferson continued to give primacy to agriculture. In 1803, not for the first time, Jefferson voiced the fear that there was 'too strong a current from the country to the towns' in the USA, with some signs of the 'sinks of voluntary misery' that constituted European towns attracting people who sought 'to live by their heads rather than their hands'. In 1804, he wrote: 'we should allow its just weight to the moral and physical preference of the agricultural, over the manufacturing, man.'[24] Many of the founding fathers shared to varying extents the outlook of Jefferson, which would exclude American Indians and slaves along with city mobs from self-governing society. 'Democracy' was at this time something to be avoided rather than pursued.

Another prominent American, Noah Webster of dictionary fame, lighted in 1785 on a craftsman made famous by Adam Smith, before giving emphasis to farmers:

A man who makes heads of pins or springs of watches, spends his days in that manufacture and never looks beyond it. This manner of fabricating things for the use and convenience of life is the means of perfecting the arts; but it cramps the human mind, by confining all its faculties to a point. In countries thinly inhabited, or where people live principally by agriculture, as in America, every man is in some measure an artist – he makes a variety of utensils, rough indeed, but such as will answer his purpose – he is a husbandman in summer and a mechanic in winter – he travels about the country – he converses with a variety of professions – he reads public papers – he has access to a parish library and thus becomes acquainted with history and politics, and every man in New England is a theologian. This will always be the case in America, so long as there is a vast tract of fertile land to be cultivated, which will occasion emigrations from the states already settled. Knowledge is diffused and genius roused by the very situation of America.[25]

By no means all educated Americans shared the outlook of Thomas Jefferson and Noah Webster. A powerful spokesman for the contrary view was Alexander Hamilton, as in, for example, his 'Report on Manufactures' that he composed as secretary of the treasury in 1790. He argued with his own emphasis that 'the mere separation of the occupation of the cultivator, from that of the Artificer, has the effect of augmenting the *productive powers* of labor, and with them, the total mass of the produce or revenue of a Country.'[26] Without such a division of labour, the USA would be dependent on the more advanced countries of Europe. And Hamilton had already made clear his view of Europe during the great debate on the acceptance of the Federal Constitution of 1787:

> The world may politically, as well as geographically, be divided into four parts, each having a distinct set of interests. Unhappily for the other three, Europe, by her arms and by her negotiations, by force and fraud, has, in different degrees, extended her dominion over them all. Africa, Asia, and America, have successively felt her domination. The superiority she has long maintained has tempted her to plume herself as the Mistress of the World, and to consider the rest of mankind as created for her benefit... It belongs to us to vindicate the honor of the human race, and to teach that assuming brother, moderation.[27]

With the onset of the French Revolution in 1789, most of Hamilton's fellow countrymen came to share his view of Europe.

As the French Revolution was arriving, a discerning Englishman took a close look at its onset. The essential message of Arthur Young's *Travels in France*, taking place in 1787, 1788 and 1789, was conveyed in two of his observations: 'The magic of property turns sand to gold'; and 'Whenever you stumble upon a grand seigneur, even one that is worth millions, you are sure to find his property desert'. In other words, he was in favour of a stimulus to peasant–tenant agriculture and against the absentee landowning nobility. Young concluded that: 'The American revolution has laid the foundation of another in France, if government does not take care of itself.'[28]

Of course, there were considerable differences between events in the USA following 1776 and France following 1789, largely stemming from the differences between a more flexible and a more rigid society. Moreover, because of European world dominance in the late eighteenth century, the French Revolution gave the rights of man the widest possible publicity, and made a signal contribution to the development of the vocabulary of modern politics. And the European context was significant in another way: across the Atlantic, the American Revolution benefited from foreign intervention; at the heart of a monarchical continent, the French Revolution was hampered by it.

Enlightenment and Intellectual Revolutions

We cannot follow the course of the French Revolution any more than we could that of its American predecessor. Instead, we will concentrate on some examples of the works produced under the influence of these revolutions and of the Enlightenment, the great intellectual movement which we will also leave without overall assessment. In hiding and in fear of his life, the Marquis de Condorcet wrote his *Esquisse d'un tableau historique des progrès de l'esprit humain* (1793–4). His study of the past convinced him that three tendencies would continue in the future: the destruction of inequality between nations; the destruction of inequality between classes; and the improvement of individuals, indeed the perfectibility of human nature – intellectually, morally and physically. Among successors influenced by Condorcet's enunciation of a science of society were Auguste Comte, Charles Darwin and Karl Marx, whose work we shall examine in the next chapter.

More immediately, Thomas Malthus's *An essay on the Principle of Population as it affects the Future Improvement of Society, with Remarks on the Speculations of Mr. Godwin, M. Condorcet, and other Writers* was published in 1798. Like Condorcet, William Godwin believed in progress, even perfectibility, as he argued in *The Inquiry concerning Political Justice, and its Influence on General Virtue and Happiness*, published in 1793. Malthus, taking a more pessimistic view, argued that 'population increases in a geometrical, food in an arithmetical ratio'. While war, disease and poverty would help to restrict the growth of population, ultimately the only countervailing force to population growth would be moral restraint. Here was an argument that would appeal to the better-fed members of society, absolving them of responsibility for the hunger of their less fortunate fellows. In America, Thomas Jefferson was not alone in thinking that virtuous farmers would avoid the problem of too little food for too many mouths. But Malthus argued that there could be no 'perpetual youth' in America: one 'might as well reasonably expect to prevent a wife or mistress from growing old by never exposing her to the sun and air.' Like Condorcet, Malthus would also influence the work of Comte, Darwin and Marx.[29]

Let us turn to the study of history in the Enlightenment. In 1744, the third and final edition of Giambattista Vico's *Scienza Nuova* was published (also known in translation as *The Principles of a New Science concerning the Common Nature of Nations*). Vico's work described how, beginning as 'stupid, insensate, and horrible beasts', men developed through three historical ages – of the gods, heroes and men. During the first age, men 'thought everything was a god or was made or done by a god'. In the second age, might was right, and heroic was virtually synonymous with barbaric. The third age introduced reason and civilisation, albeit with some loss of the power of imagination and of the sense of the sublime. Although the *New Science* argued that the order of ideas must follow the order of institutions – 'first the forests, after that the huts, then the villages, next the cities, and finally the academies', it fell short of describing the socio-economic stages of development identified by Adam Smith and Adam Ferguson.[30]

Generally speaking, as leading authority Roy Porter has pointed out, the study of history in Europe was moving on from narratives beginning at the Creation and continuing with God's providential promotion of civilisation to expositions with a more naturalistic viewpoint. David Hume defined the historian's task thus: 'to remark the rise, progress, declension, and final extinction of the most flourishing empires: the virtues, which contributed to their greatness, and the vices which drew on their ruin.'[31] An outstanding example of such an exercise was Edward Gibbon's multivolumed *Decline and Fall of the Roman Empire* published between 1776 and 1788, beginning in the same year as the American Revolution and ending in the year before the French Revolution. Gibbon wrote:

We imperceptibly advance from youth to age without observing the gradual, but incessant, change of human affairs; and even in our larger experience of history, the imagination is accustomed, by a perpetual series of causes and effects, to unite the most distant revolutions. But if the interval between two memorable eras could be instantly annihilated; if it were possible, after a momentary slumber of two hundred years, to display the *new* world to the eyes of a spectator who still retained a lively and recent impression of the *old*, his surprise and his reflections would furnish the pleasing subject of a philosophical romance.

'Revolution', it must be said, had a narrower meaning in the eighteenth century, although not so narrow perhaps when applied to the conversion to Christianity of the Emperor Constantine, on which Gibbon commented:

> This awful revolution may be usefully applied to the instruction of the present age. It is the duty of a patriot to prefer and promote the exclusive interest and glory of his native country: but a philosopher may be permitted to enlarge his views, and to consider Europe as one great republic, whose various inhabitants have attained almost the same level of politeness and cultivation. The balance of power will continue to fluctuate, and the prosperity of our own or the neighbouring kingdoms may be alternately exalted or depressed; but these partial events cannot essentially injure our general state of happiness, the system of arts, and laws, and manners, which so advantageously distinguish, above the rest of mankind, the Europeans and their colonies. The savage nations of the globe are the common enemies of civilised society...

Gibbon added:

> From the Gulf of Finland to the Eastern Ocean, Russia now assumes the form of a powerful and civilised empire. The plough, the loom, and the forge are introduced on the banks of the Volga, the Oby, and the Lena; and the fiercest of the Tartar hordes have been taught to tremble and obey. The reign of independent barbarism is now contracted to a narrow span...

In a footnote he commented:

> America now contains about six millions of European blood and descent; and their numbers, at least in the North, are constantly increasing. Whatever may be the changes of their political situation, they must preserve the manners of Europe; and we may reflect with some pleasure that the English language will probably be diffused over an immense and populous continent.

With some reservations, he asserted:

> Since the first discovery of America, the arts, war, commerce, and religious zeal have diffused among the savages of the Old and

New World these inestimable gifts; they have been successively propagated; they can never be lost. We may therefore acquiesce in the pleasing conclusion that every age of the world has increased and still increases the real wealth, the happiness, the knowledge, and perhaps the virtue of the human race.[32]

Two hundred years back may be compared with two hundred forward, not necessarily to the advantage of the late twentieth century. Without explicitly adopting the stadial concept of human development, Gibbon undoubtedly made some incisive comments on it, in particular on the Europe contemporaneous to him as well as the Europe of classical times. He clearly observed the rise of the future superpowers, Russia and America, on the landward and transoceanic flanks of the continent.

Further light might be thrown on this subject by a consideration of the manner in which Montesquieu's great work, *The Spirit of the Laws* (1748), was received in Russia and the USA, it being used by Catherine the Great to justify her enlightened absolutism, and by James Madison and others to authenticate the Federal Constitution.[33]

The cumulative effect of all the experiences of Europe persuaded Edmund Burke to declare in 1796:

There have been periods of time in which communities apparently in peace with each other, have been more perfectly separated than, in latter times, many nations in Europe have been in the course of long and bloody wars. The cause must be sought in the similitude throughout Europe of religion, laws, and manners. At bottom, these are all the same... The whole of the polity and economy of every country in Europe has been derived from the same sources.

This observation calls for some latter-day comment. To take religion first, there is no doubt that Christianity provided the principal identifier of Europe throughout the medieval period up to the later seventeenth century, at which point it was overtaken by a secular definition exemplified by the replacement of Latin by French as the leading language of international communication. However, there was a counterculture, too. The vast majority of Europeans at the time when Burke wrote were peasants, often more preoccupied by pagan supernaturalism than by church doctrine, as unaware of French as of

Latin, and still less conscious that there was a family of Indo-European languages to which both Latin and French belonged. Nevertheless, 'outsiders' be they Moslem or Jew, even Catholic or Protestant, were often treated with harsh intolerance by the uneducated and educated alike. To turn to laws, again as well as the codified and customary common varieties, there was another, more basic kind, exemplified by the almost universal belief of the peasants that the land was theirs. Perhaps, Burke had this consideration in mind when he wrote 'the little catechism of the rights of men is soon learned'.[34] As far as manners were concerned, in the narrower sense etiquette was as yet beyond the reach of the majority. In the wider sense in which Burke meant it, that is, as the French say, *moeurs*, there was possibly more generally shared throughout the whole continent. Before the agricultural improvements of the eighteenth century, the main occupation tended to follow comparable patterns and engendered comparable outlooks. At the 'highest' level, a kind of European culture was in process of formation by the time of the French Revolution; at least there was interaction between national cultures exemplified by the influence of individuals such as Shakespeare and Cervantes. Sadly, here too, as in other spheres we have to recognise the influence of war, or at least to acknowledge that Goethe had a point when he observed that 'The first and really vital material of the higher order came into German literature through Frederick the Great and the deeds of the Seven Years War.'[35]

Burke asserted that 'No citizen of Europe could be altogether an exile in any part of it'.[36] Nevertheless, such a citizen could still feel himself completely abroad when he travelled for whatever purpose beyond Europe. On the other hand, by the time of the French Revolution, Europeans were becoming more aware of their commanding relationship with most of the rest of the world, much to the annoyance of Alexander Hamilton and other potential rivals.[37] However, a cautionary note had been struck in 1756 by Voltaire in *Essai sur l'histoire générale et sur les moeurs et l'esprit des nations*, his 'universal history' in which he attempted to describe the contribution of the world's major civilisations to its development, beginning with China. He argued that the increasing dominance of European empires did not stem from moral or cultural superiority, but from social and political systems capable of generating the necessary measure of force.

Napoleon

Nobody of his time knew how to use force like Napoleon, who is still today a towering figure in the history of France, Europe and the world. He himself argued that he was trying to unite the French, Germans, Italians and other peoples into nations that could have constituted a United States of Europe, formidable in its relations with other continents. However, he became bogged down in Spain, overstretched himself in Russia and could not defeat Great Britain. The early victories led on to the finale of Waterloo.

Bonapartism as developed by the first Napoleon became a device for staying in power, increasingly making use of censorship and police to suppress possible sources of opposition. Frédéric Bluche comments:

> What is Bonapartism at the end of the imperial experience? This is a new formula of power, combining democracy (passive) and authority (active), a 'centrist' formula founded on a composite legitimacy. It is a form of authoritarian government and of centralising administration. It is the rough draft of a simple doctrine, but it is no longer a powerful political current. And this is for want of a veritable army of supporters for the regime, outside of the army properly so called (officers, NCOs, sometimes soldiers). For the Empire... can survive only through victory. Prolonged war, in spite of the personal popularity of the emperor, contains in embryo the final defeat and collapse of the system.[38]

However, it would be wrong to finish on such a negative note confined to France at the beginning of the nineteenth century. Taking a view that is more positive, wider and longer term, Stuart Woolf suggests:

> It could be argued that the model of France, perhaps even more than that of Britain, was central in this construction of the political concept of modern Europe, precisely because in the hands of the liberals national identity was combined with the leading role attributed to the state. For one of the most remarkable features of this legacy of the Napoleonic years was the growing association of liberalism and standardizing administrative reforms as the method to forge a unified state identity... Thus it was not just the nation state as the modal political unit that Europe exported to the rest

of the world, but its particular stated version of the Napoleonic experience.[39]

Bluche and Wolfe are among the more recent contributors to a never-ending discussion. Let us emphasise this point with a glance at *Napoleon: For and Against*, a book written towards the end of the Second World War. In his original preface, the author Pieter Geyl wrote:

> When one sees the French licking the hand that chastised them; when one notices how the errors and crimes of the Hero, the trials of the people, the distances and losses of the State, were forgotten in the glamour of military achievement, of power, unsound and transitory though it was; when one notices the explanations and constructions, ingenious, imperative, grandiose, that were put up as much as a century later by historians – and such excellent historians! – then one seems already to discern among later generations of German historians the apologists and admirers of the man who was our oppressor and who led them to their ruin.

Having done time in Buchenwald, Geyl could well be forgiven for these remarks, although adding 'even when as in my case one had hated the dictator in Napoleon long before the evil presence of Hitler began darkening our lives, one almost feels as if one should ask the pardon of his shade for mentioning his name in one breath with that of the other.' Most of his book sets out the evolution of the interpretation of Napoleon through the nineteenth and twentieth centuries up to the eve of the Second World War, with many ups and downs.[40] As we shall continue to see in the rest of this book, the part played by individuals in history remains controversial.

Conclusion

Nobody alive at the time realised that greenhouse gases were forming in parts of the earth's atmosphere and that biotic assemblages were beginning to experience large changes in the earth's waters at the same time as James Watt's perfection of the steam engine. Equally, nobody alive then could foresee how the steam engine would provide the power for the Industrial Revolution to transform the world's economy and society, beginning in Europe and the USA. Certainly, Adam Smith saw how free enterprise would best lead to rapid growth and Adam Ferguson described the emergence of civil society, but both of them wrote as the farming stage in human development was moving into the commercial, some time before the Industrial Revolution was moving 'full steam ahead'. Similarly, along with most of his fellow-countrymen, Thomas Jefferson favoured farming as the American Revolution unfolded and he enunciated basic principles of human rights in pre-industrial USA (albeit with a dissentient opinion from Alexander Hamilton and his followers). Arthur Young was among those in favour of the preeminence of agriculture as the French Revolution approached.

The French Revolution aroused great hopes for the future of mankind in Condorcet and Godwin, and great apprehensions in Malthus. Meanwhile evolving at a more deliberate pace, the study of history did not quickly become a *New Science* as proposed by Vico. Gibbon described the decline and fall of the Roman Empire in a more traditional manner, although with half an eye on the changes that he appreciated in more modern Europe and North America. Burke summed-up the process that had made Europe predominant in the world by the end of the eighteenth century.

Napoleon divided Europe as he sought to unite it. The 'Little Corporal' made a great impact on posterity, too, especially in the nineteenth century. Even in the twentieth century, he still provided a prime focus for analysis of the role of the individual in history. From Watt to Napoleon, this chapter in general has consisted of a description of the contributions of individuals, although, paradoxically, the overall purpose has been to use them as illustrations of 'Enlightenment and Revolutions', of aspects of human 'progress' as a whole during the first phase of the Anthropocene Era, 1763–1815.

Chapter 3

NATIONS AND -ISMS, 1815–1871

Nations and -Isms

Throughout most of the nineteenth century, Europe continued to lead the way in the dual process of industrial advancement and pollution accelerated by James Watt's steam engine, thus leading towards the crisis that we face at the beginning of the twenty-first century. Meanwhile, the analytical approach to stages of human development adopted by Adam Smith, Adam Ferguson and others was taken forward but was also subject to some distortion.

In 1815, Napoleon was finally defeated at Waterloo. In exile at St Helena, he talked of the aims for which he had worked while in power. He said that he had tried to merge the peoples of Europe into nations joined together by 'unity of codes, principles, opinions, feelings, and interest'. He had thought of setting up a central assembly on an ancient Greek or a modern American model, to take care of 'the great European family' with the guidance and protection of his empire. In spite of his defeat, he still believed that what he had worked for would ultimately be realised.[1]

Even in the long run, Napoleon's alleged dream was to fall somewhat short of realisation. More immediately, the Congress of Vienna, on which his remarks might well have been intended as a critical comment, did very little to order the affairs of the continent in anything like the manner that he envisaged. Then, as if realising their own shortcomings, the principal signatories of the Treaty of Vienna (1815), Austria, Britain, Prussia and Russia, were soon joined by France in their attempt to maintain an order based on states and their empires throughout Europe and the world.

Their emphasis remained on restoration rather than reconstruction, however, as they made an attempt partly to go back to the Europe of the eighteenth century rather than moving fully into the nineteenth.

Monarchs and their mostly noble advisers attempted in this manner to reimpose their authority over the lower orders. Unfortunately for them, the impact of the French Revolution could not be ignored. As T. C. W. Blanning has observed:

> With amazing speed the revolutionaries created a whole new political culture, quite different in theory and practice from even the most liberal polities of Europe. Underpinned by the principle of national sovereignty, it was an ideology with a short past but a great future, for it wrapped into one explosive package the three great abstractions of modern politics – the state, the nation and the people.[2]

The non-noble orders were not prepared to revert to the old regime. In particular, the upper middle class or *grande bourgeoisie* was able to insist on a due recognition of its right to participate in government based on a consolidation of its property and wealth. An assertion of its political power was to be found in the emerging ideology of liberalism, aimed basically at protecting its interests. In its turn, the upper middle class was to find that its own newly-asserted predominance was under threat from the lower members of its own class, even more from those of the embryonic industrial proletariat, so that it was sometimes driven into alliance with the landed nobility, itself concerned by the occasional insurgence of the peasants. As for the assault on the propertied classes, while it contained traditional elements of blind fury or utopian expectation, it also moved towards a more coherent outlook that was to develop later in radical directions. Socialism was to join liberalism as an emerging ideology. To be sure, social structure as well as ideology varied from one part of the continent to the other: generally speaking, the bourgeoisie and the proletariat were less to be found the further to the east, according to a slower pace of industrial revolution. With a similar regulator, across the Atlantic a looser kind of social structure and a democratic ideology were in process of formation in the USA.

Indeed, as ever, the history of Europe was affected during the years from 1815 to 1848 by events unfolding in the world beyond. In this period, a special place is occupied by the Americas, where independence movements stemming from the experience of the USA and of revolutionary France were to weaken further the empires of Spain and Portugal. Back in Europe, the decline of the Ottoman Empire also made it difficult to maintain the settlement of 1815 in its original condition. The struggle for Greek independence assumed special significance. But perhaps the most compelling imperative towards political change was the continuance and spread of industrial revolution.

This became evident in the revolution of 1848, which shook society throughout Europe, including a stronger bourgeoisie and a nascent proletariat. Admittedly, the revolution was more in thought than in deed, more in debate than in blood. As a consequence, some progress was made towards parliamentary democracy. However, greater impetus was given to nationalism, for example in Germany and Italy, which both achieved unification by 1871, when Germany was to replace France as the leading power on the continent of Europe. 1848 also marked the birth of Marxism.

In the wider world after 1848, Britain extended its informal empire in Asia, and suppressed the Indian Rebellion of 1857, after which India was incorporated in the formal empire. Self-government was extended to New Zealand, the Australian states and Canada. France was primarily interested in North and West Africa and Southeast Asia. Germany, Italy and other states began to expand beyond their boundaries. In particular, Russia consolidated its empire into central Asia and the Far East, where Vladivostok was founded by 1860. By this time, having rounded out its boundaries at the expense of the American Indians, the USA was on the eve of its civil war. That great event prepared the ground for further internal development and fresh external expansion. Japan emerged from its slumber with the Meiji Restoration of 1868, while China remained a sleeping giant open to the infiltration of the Western great powers, which retained their overall superiority in weapons of war.

Monarchism, Nationalism, Liberalism

In a secret memorandum to Alexander I of Russia in 1820, the Austrian chancellor Metternich considered that the sole function of a statesman was to 'prop up mouldering institutions', in particular monarchy. In his view, man's nature was immutable, apparent differences being brought about by influences mostly geographical. On such a basis, institutions might come and go, but two elements were indestructible: 'the precepts of morality, religious as well as social, and the necessities created by locality'. Unfortunately, 'presumption' made every man substitute individual conviction for faith and consider himself to be 'the arbiter of laws according to which he is pleased to govern himself, or to allow some one else to govern him and his neighbours'. It was mostly the middle classes of society that had been affected by this 'moral gangrene'; mostly wealthy men, whose rallying cry since 1815 had been 'Constitution', who had provoked agitation. This might mean different things in different countries, but everywhere meant 'change and trouble'.

Yet in Germany and elsewhere, Metternich claimed, the great mass of the people asked only for peace and quiet. They wanted laws protecting individuals, families and property, and dreaded any threat to such stability. Acting according to such general wishes, governments should not be immobile; indeed they should demonstrate respect for 'the progressive development of institutions in lawful ways'. But, not giving aid or succour to 'partisans' under any disguise, they must set up a league against factions. Metternich declared: 'Union between the monarchs is the basis of the policy which must now be followed to save society from total ruin.' Threats of destruction had always existed, but the present age 'by the single fact of the liberty of the press, possesses more than any preceding age the means of contact, seduction, and attraction whereby to act on these different classes of men.' Before the latter half of the seventeenth century, liberty of the press was unknown in the world; until the end of the eighteenth century it was restrained everywhere, one of the few exceptions being Britain – 'a part of Europe separated from the continent by the sea, as well as by her language and her peculiar manners'. Through control of the press and restriction of concessions to political parties, as well as minute attention to financial affairs and the strict maintenance of religious principles, monarchs demonstrated that they were just, but strong; doing good, but being strict.[3]

Metternich could not hold back the tide, although monarchy persisted where it coalesced with a force that was growing in strength as the nineteenth century wore on – nationalism. Germany was united by nationalism of three kinds: economic, political and cultural. The idea was most powerfully expressed by Georg Wilhelm Friedrich Hegel, who wrote that 'Truth is the Unity of the universal and subjective Will; and the Universal is to be found in the State, in its laws, its universal and rational arrangements. The State is the Divine Idea as it exists on Earth.' Moreover, Hegel had no difficulty in identifying the locus for the development of the State in Germany and beyond: 'Europe is absolutely the end of history', although as its continuator 'America is therefore the land of the future'. As for the individual, be he 'world-historical Hero' or rank and file, he would fulfil his destiny via the state.[4]

In Italy, the idea preceded the reality, for only 2.5 per cent of the people in 1860 spoke what was to become the national language. Nearly thirty years before then, Mazzini was prepared to assert broadly in his General Instructions for the Members of Young Italy in 1831 that:

> The strength of an association lies, not in the numerical cypher of the elements of which it is composed, but in the homogeneousness of those elements; in the perfect concordance of its members as to the path to be followed, and the certainty that the moment of action will find them ranged in a compact phalanx, strong in reciprocal trust, and bound together by unity of will, beneath a common banner.

Moreover, in his view, there was already underway 'a progressive series of transformations which are gradually and irresistibly guiding European society to form itself into vast and united masses'. Yet Mazzini's aim – a republican, unitarian Italy – and the means that he recommended to reach it – education and insurrection – were expounded in a manner that fitted the particular rather than the general case. Moreover, Mazzini asserted, if 'God has written one line of his thought on the cradle of each people', Italy was 'the land destined by God to the great mission of giving moral unity to Europe, and through Europe to Humanity.'[5] Almost by definition, other writers on nationalism would assign to their own nation a similarly superior role. Hence one of the greatest difficulties in writing a history of the continent: if full allowance were made for the self-image of each and every nation, the work would never be finished!

We may make a clear distinction between those states that were already in existence at the beginning of the nineteenth century, and those that were as yet nothing more than the glimmer in the eye of a few intellectuals. On the whole, with Italy a major exception, the west of the continent fits into the first category, although composed of amalgams of numbers of earlier independent units. In the centre and east of the continent, there were many peoples subject to the

Austro-Hungarian, Russian and Ottoman empires. Some of them, for example, in Bulgaria and Romania, were soon to be given a new affiliation. But peasants, who predominated in these new states, were far less conscious of their nation than city dwellers. Even in the early twentieth century, according to one calculation, about 90 per cent of those living in what was to become Ukraine had little or no awareness of it.[6]

However, although there are artificial aspects to all nation states, we may be ill-advised to accept the notion that they are all inventions. Even if nationalism flares up and dies down in a somewhat fickle flame, such a powerful emotion cannot be dismissed.

Often allied with nationalism, liberalism was such a powerful force because it was associated with economic as well as political development. For example, the German Friedrich List argued that Adam Smith and his contemporaries had given insufficient attention to the necessity for nationalism. He wrote of Britain and its system of free trade that: 'It is a rule of elementary prudence, when you have reached the top, to kick away the ladder you have used, in order to deprive the others of the means of climbing up after you.' Free trade might be 'very desirable' but it was not the condition of 'the actual world'. Other nations needed to resort to tariffs to protect their trade, until they were strong enough to open their commercial doors to outside rivals. In order to achieve the necessary progress, these nations should take legislative and administrative steps to ensure that agriculture, industry and commerce were combined in harmonious proportions. Moreover, unlike Smith, who had insisted on the preeminence of agriculture, List argued that phases of economic growth culminated in industry. In general, he asserted, German and much other continental economic liberalism, as well as American, should differ considerably from the major British model.[7]

Similarly, the extent to which political ideas and groups should follow the example set by the French in the years following 1789 was debated with much passion. In France itself, for example, Benjamin Constant in his *Principles of Politics* (1815) attacked the power of the state, with the all too clear knowledge of what Napoleon had done with it fresh in his mind: Bonaparte, he wrote, was 'a thousand times' more guilty than 'barbarous conquerors'. Popular sovereignty had its limits, but was the best guarantor of man's divine attribute of freedom: 'encompassing the sovereignty of the people within its just limits, you have nothing to fear.'[8] Alexis de Tocqueville argued on the basis of the experiences that he analysed in *Democracy in America*, published in 1835, that 'a nation may establish a system of free government, but without the spirit of municipal institutions it cannot have the spirit of liberty.' Generally speaking, he believed that democracy would spread from the USA to Europe.[9]

In Britain, James Mill was more than anybody the founder of 'philosophic radicalism', moving from support for the rights of man towards the argument that good government could best be secured by a wide extension of the franchise. He was also a devoted disciple of Jeremy Bentham, who believed that his ideas of Utilitarianism, 'the Greatest Happiness of the Greatest Number', were best guaranteed through emphasising the rights of the individual and free trade. On the other hand, John Stuart Mill, son of James, while accepting the importance of the individual, also asserted that state intervention was necessary to secure Utilitarian ends, that the state should encourage cooperative enterprises and reduce inequality by curbing rights of inheritance. But he stopped short of socialism. Indeed, liberalism allowed a wide range of interpretation, partly because of explicit definition, partly because of implicit definition. That is to say, liberalism was taken to be not only open ended but was also the inherent ideology of free-born men everywhere, especially in Britain and the USA.[10]

Socialism

'When Adam delved and Eve span, who was then the gentleman?' was a rallying cry during the English Peasant Revolt of 1381. The Levellers in seventeenth-century England and the followers of Babeuf in late-eighteenth-century France were among the forerunners of a movement that, like nationalism, received new definition in the nineteenth century.

Then, a comprehensive attempt to include society as a whole, especially industrial society, was made by writers espousing the doctrines of 'socialism', a word that gained coinage in the 1830s. Its first adherents were such propagandists as Robert Owen, who attempted to set up a model community at New Lanark near Glasgow in Scotland; the Comte de Saint-Simon, who argued for a 'New Christianity' led by men of science and bringing capital and labour together in harmony; and F. M. Charles Fourier, who sought a 'new industrial world' composed of communes. These two Frenchmen and their British counterpart were deemed by their more renowned successor, the German Karl Marx, to be 'critical-Utopian', that is, capable of perceiving what the problems of society were, but unable to provide appropriate solutions. Together with his close associate Friedrich Engels, the German manufacturer of textiles in Manchester, England, Marx at the beginning of the revolution of 1848 set about writing the *Manifesto of the Communist Party*, the original statement of the ideology that was to become known as Marxism. In view of Marxism's later importance as the 'scientific' antithesis of liberalism, the *Manifesto* deserves extended exposition.[11]

The brief introduction describes the growing power of the ideology: 'A spectre is haunting Europe – the spectre of Communism. All the powers of old Europe have entered into a holy alliance to exorcise this spectre...' It was high time, the introduction continues, that the Communists assembling in London should set out in their various languages their views, aims and tendencies in order to meet 'this nursery tale of the Spectre of Communism with a manifesto of the party itself'.[12]

The Manifesto then begins its first section, entitled 'Bourgeois and Proletarians', with a description of its basic assertion: 'The history of all hitherto existing society is the history of class struggles.' After their development through the ancient and medieval periods, those struggles were now taking on the simple shape of two great hostile camps consisting of two great classes – the bourgeoisie, or capitalist owners, and the proletariat, or wage labourers who owned nothing but their ability to work which they sold in order to live. The discovery of America and the opening up of wider commercial possibilities in general led, along with steam and machinery, to the establishment of modern industry and the world market, and to the intensification of the class struggle.

Historically, the bourgeoisie had played a most revolutionary part, replacing old social ties with the naked self-interest of a relationship based on cash. In other words: 'for exploitation, veiled by religious and political illusions, it has substituted naked, shameless, direct, brutal exploitation.' And yet: 'It has been the first to show what man's activity can bring about. It has accomplished wonders far surpassing Egyptian pyramids, Roman aqueducts and Gothic cathedrals; it has conducted expeditions that put in the shade all former exoduses of nations and crusades.' During the demonstration of its accomplishments:

> The bourgeoisie has subjected the country to the rule of the towns. It has created enormous cities, has greatly increased the urban populations as compared with the rural, and has thus rescued a considerable part of the population from the idiocy of rural life. Just as it has made the country dependent on the towns, so it has made barbarian and semi-barbarian countries dependent on the civilised ones, nations of peasants on nations of bourgeois, the East on the West.

Marx and Engels showed here that they shared the prejudices of their contemporaries concerning the Ancient and Middle Ages, provincial existence and the world beyond Europe, moving on from the partiality for rural life shared by Smith, Ferguson and Jefferson. Possibly, they celebrated the achievements of the bourgeoisie in too lyrical a manner. However, they also believed that they had discerned more clearly than others the manner in which the very success of capitalism would lead to the downfall of the bourgeoisie, which was 'like the sorcerer, who is no longer able to control the powers of the nether world whom he has called up by his spells'. For 'the weapons with which the bourgeoisie felled feudalism to the ground are now turned against the bourgeoisie itself'.[13] The necessity for ever improved methods of production in an increasingly competitive market would mean the breaking of national barriers and the daily destruction of old-established industries that would not adapt themselves to such changing demands. For a few to succeed in such a fierce struggle, many would have to fail. The large capitalists would swamp the small, and thus from all classes of the population would be recruited the mortal enemy of the bourgeoisie – the proletariat.

Workers became enmeshed in capitalism through the sale of the only cash commodity at their disposal: their ability to work. They became appendages of the machines of industry, and were crowded into factories like soldiers. Paradoxically, however, their abject humiliation led to the formation of their strength. Herded together under strict regimentation, the workers developed their class consciousness and their own organisations or unions. This process occurred more quickly and in more strained national and international circumstances than the preceding process of the emergence of the bourgeoisie. Because of the pace of change and the associated difficulties, each national bourgeoisie was obliged 'to appeal to the proletariat, to ask for its help, and thus to drag it into the political arena', not only to complete the struggle against the old order but also to fight with the rival bourgeoisies of foreign countries. Willy-nilly, the bourgeoisie helped the proletariat to prepare itself for the struggle between the two classes: 'The bourgeoisie, therefore, supplies the proletariat with its own elements of political and general education, in other words, it furnishes the proletariat with weapons for fighting the bourgeoisie.'

The proletariat would receive further assistance from bourgeois-becoming proletarians and from bourgeois ideologists able to understand in a theoretical manner the historical process as a whole. Some of these would become Communists, providing general explanations of what the workers had learned through their collective experience. Without property and without family relations based on property, the workers were stripped of every trace of national character, in Britain as in France, in the USA as in Germany. Thus, the workers had no country, while national differences and antagonisms were 'daily more and more vanishing, owing to the development of the bourgeoisie, to freedom of commerce, to the world market, to uniformity in the mode of production and in the conditions of life corresponding thereto.' When the proletariat had consolidated its position, class distinctions would disappear, too, and public power would lose its political character, since 'political power, properly so called, is merely the organised power of one class for oppressing another'. The new order would consist of 'an association, in which the free development of each is the condition for the free development of all'.[14]

There is no doubt that Marx and Engels, while standing on the shoulders of Owen, Saint-Simon, Fourier and other predecessors, such as G. W. F. Hegel as well as Adam Smith and Adam Ferguson, had established an interpretation of history which was much more comprehensive or, in the wider sense of the term, scientific. However, a stumbling block to the realisation of their projections in the short run would be the persistence of that phenomenon which they saw as temporary or transient – nationalism, in particular as a reflection of economic and social change. Erroneously, they believed that a forthcoming bourgeois revolution in Germany would be immediately followed by a proletarian revolution there because the conditions in which it would occur would be much more advanced than those of its predecessors in Britain and France.

Just over twenty years on, the bourgeois revolution did indeed occur in Germany to the extent that the process of unification was complete with the creation of the German Empire in 1871. No proletarian revolution was to follow, however much it was worked and yearned for by the members of the Communist International and others. However appealing to millions throughout the world, the proletarian revolution and the ensuing communist society were predictions that added a utopian element to an incisive analysis. In this sense, while transcending the legacy of Smith and Ferguson concerning stadial development, Marx and Engels also distorted it. Moreover, by the time of Marx's death in 1883, in his uncompleted major work, *Capital*, he had shown in some detail how capitalism was on the rise, but had not spelled out in such detail how it was to fall, still less what was to replace it. His great achievement was to analyse the process by which the development of technology far beyond the dreams of James Watt promoted a new economic system and accompanying social changes. However, he could not foresee the extent to which a managerial, technocratic stratum would become a substantial part of the bourgeoisie, and the manner in which a substantial part of the proletariat would become integrated into a consumer, service economy. The debate about the sequel would continue as socialism, both Marxist and non-Marxist, gained vigour as the antithesis of liberalism while nationalism was reinforced by imperialism. As yet, whatever the -ism, there was little realisation that all-round disaster would ensue from the belief that nature could be exploited and controlled.

Darwinism and Other -Isms

In 1859, Charles Darwin published *The Origin of Species*. He was prompted by his realisation that Alfred Russel Wallace had come to conclusions very similar to his own. Moreover, he not only made use of his own lengthy and detailed research but also drew on the research of others on a wide range of subjects from the study of fossils (in particular by Charles Lyell) and micro-organisms (especially by Louis Pasteur and Joseph Lister) to economics and sociology (including Malthus). *The Origin of Species*, then, was not a bolt from the blue. Darwin put forward the argument that all living species had evolved through adaptation to their environment: the struggle for survival had led to natural selection, some species adapting successfully, others failing. Darwin's bold propositions came at a time of great confidence in science, but also helped to provoke opposition to it. By the time of publication of *The Descent of Man* in 1871, church leaders and others were putting forward passionate objections. To collect fossils and make suggestions about their categories was one thing; to assert that human beings themselves were part of a vast process involving all life-forms was another.

A further blow to convention came from Darwin's confirmation of the extension of time itself. In the early nineteenth century, in spite of arguments to the contrary by James Hutton and others, the belief was still widespread that the earth had been created some six thousand years previously. On the other hand, Darwin himself wrote in the conclusion of *The Origin of Species*: 'The whole history of the world, as at present known, although of a length quite incomprehensible by us, will hereafter be recognised as a mere fragment of time, compared with the ages which have elapsed since the first creature, the progenitor of innumerable extinct and living descendants, was created.' He saw vistas opening for researches in psychology, with light thrown on the origin and history of humankind.[15]

The vast process included what was to become known as 'Social Darwinism', of which the great man's major biographers write that it is 'often taken to be something extraneous, an ugly concretion added to the pure Darwinian corpus after the event, tarnishing Darwin's image.' However, Desmond and Moore continue, 'his notebooks make plain that competition, free trade, imperialism, racial extermination, and sexual inequality were written into the equation from the start – "Darwinism" was always intended to explain human society.' We shall note the impact of 'Social Darwinism' in the next chapter, where it will be seen to give authority to ideas of progress.[16]

Other -isms, including feudalism and absolutism, were devised to describe earlier developments. Since the present was messier than the past, however, the -isms adopted to describe further aspects of what was going on in the nineteenth century itself were often inexact. We cannot do without these terms, but equally we cannot be as precise as we would like in our use of them.

To take one further important example, there might be wide agreement that Romanticism was in part promoted by the French Revolution and Napoleon. According to one of many definitions within 'a chaos of rival and competing Romanticisms', it emerged in 'a Europe recovering from a French domination which could pretend to universal progress and rationality'. In contrast, 'Romantics aimed to uncover a national character and even "racial" continuities through which the past, embodied in living memory, could speak to, guide, and nurture the present'. Moreover, Romantics 'conjured up myths of the glories of the past, the drama of the inner self as hero, spiritual voyages into the religious and the transcendental, and a communion with the mountains'. Living writers became 'a new priesthood' exerting 'a cultural influence hitherto unthinkable'. Among their contributions was an encouragement of patriotism and nationalism.[17]

As the 'chaos' of Romanticism continued to unfold, there were significant developments at the more ordered opposite end of the spectrum of human thought. The English word 'scientist' was coined in 1833 by the English philosopher William Whewell, who observed the tendency of the sciences towards separate specialisation, from amateur towards professional research, while also suggesting the possibility of their 'consilience' or compatibility of inductions – 'a test of the Truth of the Theory in which it occurs'.[18] In his *Cours de philosophie positive*, completed in six volumes by 1842, the Frenchman Auguste Comte suggested that six sciences – mathematics, astronomy, physics, chemistry, biology, sociology – had reached their third and final, positive stage (after fictional and abstract stages).[19] Positivism was to enter the vocabulary of intellectual discourse. Yet Henry Thomas Buckle was 'the first to have raised history to a science' according to an English admirer. Buckle himself wrote that he had been 'long convinced that the progress of every people is regulated by principles – or, as they are called, Laws – as regular and as certain as those which govern the physical world.' He observed with his own emphases: 'The object of all science is to rise from proximate causes to more remote ones, while in practice (which concerns the individual, and deals, not with the *science*, but with the *art* of life) the safest course is to look at what is proximate. Therefore I hold that in the former case the intellectual laws are supreme; in the latter case the moral laws.' Consequently, 'in the *long run* (or on the great average of affairs) individuals count for nothing.' Unfortunately, Buckle died before he was able to come near to realising his great vision, completing no more than a two-volume *History of Civilization in England*, published in 1857 and 1861.[20]

In 1843, Commissioner Henry L. Ellsworth of the United States Patent Office concluded a report to Congress with the observation that 'The advancement of the [mechanical] arts, from year to year, taxes our credulity and seems to presage the arrival of that period when human improvement must end.'[21] Similarly, no less a figure than Prince Albert, the patron of the British Great Exhibition of 1851, observed in 1850:

> Nobody...who has paid any attention to the particular features of our present era, will doubt for a moment that we are living at a period of the most wonderful transition, which tends to the accomplishment of that great end to which, indeed, all history points – the realization of the unity of mankind.[22]

In contrast, a 'Paris Guide' produced for the French Universal Exhibition of 1867 wrote of 'the opening of a new era', declaring:

> World exhibitions are a part of that vast economic progress which includes railways, the electric telegraph, steam navigation, the piercing of isthmuses and all those great public works, all the discoveries of science, and which will bring an increase in moral welfare, that is, more freedom, as well as an increase in material welfare, that is more affluence, to the benefit of the majority.[23]

History and Historians

To what extent did the 'the discoveries of science' include history? A first answer here is that approaches to the 'science' of history could vary considerably, under the often overlapping headings of monarchism, liberalism, nationalism, socialism, Darwinism, Romanticism and positivism, among others. For example, Karl Marx himself asked Charles Darwin for permission to make him the dedicatee of *Capital*. Darwin rejected the request, but this could not prevent Marx from thinking of history as a global evolutionary process. Indeed, he thought in this manner before the publication of *The Origin of Species* in *The Communist Manifesto*, and in later works on aspects of the revolutions of 1848 and their sequel – especially in France.

Jules Michelet's work on the French Revolution of 1789 persuaded a more recent distinguished specialist on the subject, Georges Lefebvre, to consider his predecessor the 'greatest national historian'.[24] Learning in the 1820s from his eighteenth-century predecessor Vico that 'The nature of things is nothing other than that they come into being at certain times and in certain ways' and that there were 'the specific phases and the regular process by which the customs that gave rise to law originally came into being', Michelet went on from 1830 to argue that while Christianity had given the world the moral gospel, France should preach the social gospel. He celebrated Joan of Arc not so much as an active Christian as an inspired patriot. Turning to the French Revolution, he argued that 'at no other time have distinctions of class, of fortune and of party been more completely forgotten.' Combining his sense of the organic nature of society with an appreciation of the personality of individuals involved in the great events, Michelet went on to complete his magnificent multivolumed *History of the Revolution*. On the eve of the Franco–Prussian War of 1870–1, he signed an international pacifist manifesto with Marx and Engels, but he stopped short of socialism. He noted before he died in 1874 that, born during French Revolutionary terror, he had lived to see what he called the terror of the Communist International. The history of the nineteenth century, he suggested, could be summed up in three -isms: industrialism, militarism and socialism.[25]

Thomas Babington Macaulay's *History of England* (1848) was concerned with the so-called 'Glorious and Bloodless Revolution' of 1688 – which overthrew Stuart paternalist absolutism – along with its sequel, and much more besides. In the authoritative appraisal of Owen Dudley Edwards, the real purpose of Macaulay was 'to absorb his readers in the past in its totality, absorbing above all its culture' and thus 'devising the means by which the future would show its title to rule'.[26] He was anxious to show that the complete victory of any political force would lead to the destruction of social harmony. Macaulay himself wrote of his intentions in writing the *History*:

I shall trace the course of that revolution which terminated the long struggle between our sovereigns and their parliaments, and bound up together the rights of the people and the title of the reigning dynasty. I shall relate how the new settlement was, during many troubled years, successfully defended against foreign and domestic enemies; how, under that settlement, the authority of law and the security of property were found to be compatible with a liberty of discussion and of individual action never before known;

how, from the auspicious union of order and freedom, sprang a prosperity of which the annals of human affairs had furnished no example...

However, disasters, crimes and follies had to be recorded, too. Thus, in general:

> It will be seen that the system which effectively secured our liberties against the encroachments of kingly power gave birth to a new class of abuses from which absolute monarchies are exempt. It will be seen that, in consequence partly of unwise interference, and partly of unwise neglect, the increase of wealth and the extension of trade produced, together with immense good, some evils from which poor and rude societies are free.

In particular, 'imprudence and obstinacy broke the ties which bound the North American colonies to their parent state.'[27]

As opposed to the limited, constitutional monarchy of Great Britain, the absolutist variety was to be found predominantly in Central and Eastern Europe. An outstanding apologist for Russian autocracy was Nikolai Karamzin, who produced a *Memoir on Ancient and Modern Russia* in 1811 and a multivolumed *History of the Russian State* from 1818 to 1829. Both the *Memoir*, specifically for Alexander I, and the *History*, for the tsar's successors in general, were composed with a didactic patriotic purpose clearly in mind. Karamzin argued that the Russian variety of monarchy had made the empire great and that only its vigorous continuance would avert such evils as 'the deceased French Revolution' that remains as 'a locust' from which 'nasty insects crawl out'. The heroes of the *History* were the tsars themselves up to Mikhail, the first Romanov, at whose accession in 1613 the work comes to an end. In the *Memoir*, Karamzin praises Peter the Great for the consolidation of autocracy, but criticises him for making Russia European, commenting: 'We became citizens of the world but ceased in certain respects to be citizens of Russia. The fault is Peter's.'[28]

In Karamzin's appraisal, like republican France, the USA had been created by force, and thus bound itself to a history of violence and tyranny. This was the antithesis of the interpretation published as *History of the United States* in the 1830s by George Bancroft, who was rated by his fellow-countryman William M. Sloane at the beginning of the twentieth century 'as an American historian second to none of his European contemporaries'. Bancroft, Sloane declared, 'displayed the heroic, epic value of American history, its unity with the great central stream, and dispelled for ever the extravagant conceptions of a sentimental world just emerging from the visionary philosophy of the eighteenth century.' Like most of his contemporaries, Bancroft was heavily under the influence of the German Leopold von Ranke.

Above all, Ranke has been credited with the development of the study of history as a professional 'science'. For him, this approach meant the scrupulous examination of sources and a dispassionate analysis of them. The activity of every individual and institution had to be interpreted in relation to the age in which they were to be found. Best known for his assertion of history 'as it actually was', however, Ranke also believed in a divinely ordered world in which the great powers were 'spiritual substances… Thoughts of God.'[29]

Through more than two-thirds of the nineteenth century, most Western writers of history were not professional. Demarcation lines between disciplines were not as clear as they later became. Moreover, to apply some labels to historians may be misleading. Hayden White has gone so far as to deny such designations as 'liberal' entirely, and to substitute in their place the term 'linguistic protocols'.[30] Nevertheless, the writers we have selected as representative of their age were all devoted to some cause, and this commitment needs to be recognised beyond their typification according to literary tropes.

Conclusion

The -isms on which we have concentrated in this chapter expanded the approach of the Enlightenment. The stadial analysis of Adam Smith and Adam Ferguson in particular was updated as the Industrial Revolution took human society into a new phase of development beyond the commercial, increasingly involving other parts of the world in the transformation spearheaded by Europe and the USA.

Of course, most famously in *The Communist Manifesto*, Marx and Engels discussed the role of the bourgeoisie and the proletariat, adding to the social structure established by Smith and Ferguson. However, they went beyond analysis to the prediction of a proletarian revolution to follow the bourgeois. Apprehension concerning this eventuality was to persuade some critics to throw out the achievement of the

Enlightenment along with its Marxist supplement – a great blow to the study of history as a science in addition to the blows inflicted by other -isms, in particular nationalism, and its extension – imperialism. Moreover, while progressive as natural science, and supportive of the stadial approach to the study of human society, the Darwinist concept of natural selection, especially as 'survival of the fittest', also had a negative impact in the period following 1871, as we shall soon see.

As far as the role of the individual is concerned, Napoleon's image began to fade as the nineteenth century wore on. Napoleon I was the last great man for Carlyle in 1840. His nephew, Napoleon III, was the butt of Karl Marx's scorn following the revolution of 1848, as he seemed to show 'how the class struggle in France created circumstances and relationships that made it possible for a grotesque mediocrity to play a hero's part.' After observing that the two Napoleons illustrated how history repeats itself, first as tragedy, then as farce, Marx went on to observe:

> Men make their own history, but they do not make it just as they please; they do not make it under circumstances chosen by themselves, but under circumstances directly found, given and transmitted from the past. The tradition of all the dead generations weighs like a nightmare on the brain of the living.[31]

However, this tradition could inspire a dream as well as weigh like a nightmare, for example for Bismarck in Germany. He himself said that the task of German unification would have to be completed by 'blood and iron', which the British economist Lord Keynes amended to 'coal and iron'. However, along with the Industrial Revolution, we should include the cultural, adding 'pen and ink' and voice as the widespread German language made its contribution to the ultimate success. With his consummate political skill, Bismarck was no doubt an appropriate man for the task, but, equally, he was at the right time in the right place.

Chapter 4

NATURAL SELECTION, 1871–1921

The New Imperialism

The phase of the Anthropocene Era from 1871 to 1914 may be looked upon as the period of the 'New Imperialism', as the great powers struggled to carve up the rest of the world between them before the showdown of the First World War, and of the Russian Revolution – internal instability was another of the period's distinguishing features. Joseph Chamberlain was to talk at the turn of the century of his vision of an empire for the common man, of a broad patriotism that would maintain harmony between the classes, and similar remarks were made elsewhere. Thus, historians have put forward the idea of 'social imperialism' – the pursuit of a vigorous foreign policy with at least the partial aim of providing a safety valve for domestic discontent. At the time there was much talk too, following Darwin, of the 'survival of the fittest' at home and abroad.

There are a number of other features of the 'New Imperialism'. A second industrial revolution of steel, oil, electricity and large-scale organisation began to push capitalism beyond national borders much more than before. Much of the investment and accompanying search for markets and raw materials was carried out in Europe itself, but more went to Africa, Asia and the Antipodes, while the largest injection of capital was in North and South America. Emigration now became a river in flood in comparison with the former modest stream as 25 million Europeans crossed the Atlantic to the USA in the last quarter of the nineteenth century, and a considerable if much smaller number moved in other directions, including Britons to outposts of empire and Russians to Siberia. Peasants throughout the continent were flocking to the towns in an internal migration that was at least as significant for 'social imperialism' as external migration was for imperialism in general. Governments now attempted to make their empires formal, to a large extent in order to forestall their rivals in what was a race to extend their influence throughout the world, especially in Africa and Polynesia, two regions as yet incompletely infiltrated by Europeans. The competition as well as the construction of navies steam-powered beyond the wildest dreams of James Watt made it necessary to look for bases and coaling stations, and generally to consider the manner in which maritime activity could protect imperial interests. Most European empires took on their share of 'the white man's burden', the illusion that Europeans and their emigrant relations shared a duty to bring their advanced culture including their religion to ignorant, backward peoples, some of whom at least were in fact the heirs of civilisations much older than the European, even if not so efficient in methods of exploitation and extermination.

Beyond Europe, just two powers participated in the race for empire in an active rather than a passive manner. The USA, from its ever-stronger sphere of influence in North and South America, looked increasingly outward, especially with the war against Spain in 1898 that took it into the Philippines and Cuba. The USA worked to keep the way to the Americas closed to outsiders while maintaining the 'Open Door' for all foreign nations in China and elsewhere. Japan was by this time a vigorous second non-European entrant in the race for empire, and the first non-white imperialist power, especially after its victory over Russia in 1905.

Strategic arguments for maintaining global stability fell after 1878 into two major schools, which can be conveniently linked with two names: the American naval officer Alfred T. Mahan, who wrote of the influence of sea power upon history; and Halford John Mackinder, a British geographer who gave special emphasis to the role played throughout the ages by Eurasia's 'heartland'.[1]

However, the Mahan and Mackinder arguments were probably more complementary than contradictory, the first originating in a land-based power that had comparatively neglected the sea and the other in a sea-based power that had comparatively neglected the land. Certainly, overseas imperial activity could not be separated from that taking place overland. For example, the Germany attempting to build a railway and influence from Berlin to Bagdad was no different from the Germany constructing a navy and attempting to assert itself in the North Sea and further waters. Similarly, external expansion and rivalry could not be separated from the internal tensions between the classes in all of the empires of Europe. As the history of Europe and the history of the world overlapped to an extent much greater than before, the essential connections between foreign and domestic policy remained as close as ever, and became even closer.[2]

While steam ships reduced times for sea journeys, the 'iron way' did the same on land, bringing about a revolution in chronology. Around 1870, a steam train journey from the east coast to the west coast of North America necessitated the adjustment of timepieces on more than twenty occasions. By 1884, American railroads had already agreed a more unified time system when a Prime Meridian Conference in Washington DC accepted Greenwich Time as a global standard. France held out till 1911, and Germany came in (mainly for military reasons) in 1913. Russia kept its own time and calendar until after its revolution. As Edwin A. Pratt observed in 1915 of the railways that had been constructed in Europe, North America and beyond: 'They allow of war being carried on between a number of nations at one and the same time, thus spreading the area over which the conflicts of today may extend. They encourage the cherishing of designs of world-power and dreams of universal conquest.'[3]

Such designs and dreams were encouraged by other ideas being put forward in the late nineteenth century, not only concerning the rivalry between nations and conflict between the classes but also between all life-forms. Darwin's ideas were applied to the belief that human beings banded together to ensure their own survival, and that some such groups would survive while the weaker would succumb. Thus, for example, in 1911 General F. von Bernhardi was to argue that the prospect for Germany was either world power or downfall.[4]

A process of 'natural selection' was in operation as the major European powers moved towards collision while they struggled for supereminence on the continent and for shares of the rest of the world. By around 1900 they had together risen to the peak of their global influence. But the rivalries between them were already leading by 1914 towards decline, a process to be accelerated by the emergence of the USA and Japan, and especially by the outbreak of the First World War. Together, the First World War and Russian Revolution brought European dominance to an end.

The Second Scientific and Industrial Revolution

Nationalism and imperialism played their part in the development of European science, especially after the completion of the process of Italian and German unification. Certainly, science in a united German empire was to play a bigger role than it did in the states that had constituted it. Altogether it seems possible to talk of a second scientific revolution, culminating in Einstein just as the first scientific revolution of the seventeenth century reached its climax with Newton. Let us look at some of the contributions of individuals, beginning with a general observation by one of them. In 1870, James Clerk Maxwell of Aberdeen, Edinburgh and Cambridge declared:

> It was a great step in science when men became convinced that, in order to understand the nature of things, they must begin by asking, not whether a thing is good or bad, noxious or beneficial, but of what kind is it? and how much is there of it? Quality and quantity were then first recognized as the primary features to be observed in scientific inquiry.[5]

In the years following 1871, the nature and number of scientific phenomena were indeed explored. In 1871 itself, the arrangement of the elements in order of atomic numbers in the periodic table was established by the Russian chemist Dmitrii Mendeleev. James Clerk Maxwell's electromagnetic theory of light led to the measurement of the velocity of electromagnetic waves by the German Heinrich Hertz in 1886 and the accidental discovery of X-rays in the associated area of radioactivity by another German Wilhelm Röntgen in 1895. In 1896, the Frenchman Antoine Becquerel demonstrated that uranium produced a similar sort of ray. In 1898, another Frenchman Pierre Curie and his Polish wife Marie isolated radium. (The individual contributions of Clerk Maxwell and others were recognised in the naming of units of measurement after them.) The relationship between matter and energy was being revealed, with awesome – if still to be perceived – implications for the future of warfare as well as more peaceful pursuits such as the radio, telecommunications and radiotherapy.

Generally speaking, the turn of the century marked great scientific progress, with physics still at the forefront. Two successors to Clerk Maxwell at Cambridge made great contributions to a revolutionary theory of the structure of the atom. Building on the contributions of German physicists, J. J. Thomson discovered 'corpuscles' – since known as electrons. Ernest Rutherford suggested that electrons revolved around the nucleus of the atom like planets round the sun. At the turn of the century, too, the German Max Planck put forward the theory that the energy of radiation consists of 'quanta' depending on the frequency of oscillation of the electrons. In 1905 Albert Einstein, then a patent office clerk in Bern, Switzerland, began to put forward his astounding theory of relativity, with mathematics joining physics in his description of space-time. Einstein himself observed: 'Before James Clerk Maxwell people conceived physical reality...as material points. After Maxwell they conceived physical reality as represented by continuous fields.... This change in the conception of reality is the most profound and fruitful one that has come to physics since Newton.'[6]

A significant development in chemistry was the emergence of biochemistry. In 1897, for example, the German Eduard Buchner discovered that sugar could ferment even though the accompanying crushed yeast contained no living cells. This led to the realisation not only that a dead chemical substance – the enzyme (meaning 'in yeast') – caused fermentation but that similar substances brought about most other chemical reactions taking place in living matter. As a by-product of the work on dyestuffs in German industrial laboratories, chemical pharmacology began to provide remedies for such ailments as syphilis and sleeping sickness. Another offshoot of the dyestuffs industry was the explosive trinitrotoluene (TNT), which meant termination for all the ills of those in the vicinity of its detonation, and which was often harmful to the health of those engaged in its manufacture. In biology, the Moravian Abbé Gregor Mendel had explored the processes of heredity through crossing various kinds of peas as long ago as the 1860s. However, his contribution was not fully appreciated until further contributions on heredity were made by the German August Weismann and others towards the end of the nineteenth century. Mendel was somewhat exceptional, since the other scientists listed above soon elicited a positive response from an international scientific community adopting common technologies and concepts.

We must not exaggerate the extent of the changes achieved by human beings soon after 1900. The 11th edition of the *Encyclopaedia Britannica* published in 1910–11 spoke somewhat tentatively of the aeroplane creating widespread interest 'both as a matter of sport and also as indicating a new departure in the possibilities of machines of war'. Even the land-bound motor vehicle still had some way to go before its presence in Europe ceased to be a rarity, although increasing familiarity with such vehicles meant that the British Red Flag Act (restricting their speed in towns to 2 mph and only then if accompanied by warning flags) had already become an object of ridicule since its repeal in 1896. But traffic accidents were also now common, an early fatality in Paris being Pierre Curie, the French scientist. France was at first the centre of the motor-car industry in Europe, but from 1906 the world leader was the USA, which produced nearly 115,000 cars in 1909 as opposed to just over 45,000 in France. As far as public transport was concerned, most cities in Europe possessed tramways, to an ever-increasing extent electrified, to supplement the longer distance railways, but for the most part they were confined to the major thoroughfares, beyond which horse-drawn transport was still the norm.

Developments in travel had been remarkable enough, but there had been considerable progress in other forms of communication, too. Telegraphy had first been used as an accompaniment to the railway from about 1840, but with the laying of the Atlantic cable from 1865 and of the Pacific cable from 1901 the whole world was encompassed, with many overland lines as well. Marconi began transatlantic wireless telegraphy in 1902. Meanwhile, the telephone developed in the 1870s by the Scot Alexander Graham Bell and the American Thomas Alva Edison was being used mostly in the USA, followed by Germany, Britain, France and Switzerland. While there was as yet no public broadcasting by wireless or radio, home entertainment of the traditional kind was being supplemented by the phonograph with its cylinders and the gramophone with its discs, while the cinematograph was entering the world of public entertainment, first as a music-hall turn, and then in its own right. Soon, the 'movies' or the 'flicks' would be offering a considerable challenge to the 'live' theatre, just as the still photograph had already made enough appearances in the family album to supplement the painted portrait.

While it is important to observe what Europeans and Americans did with their leisure hours at the beginning of the twentieth century, it is even more necessary to note what they did at work. For towards the end of the nineteenth century, there began the Second Industrial Revolution, with the age of coal, iron and steam joined by that of steel, electricity and oil. New materials and methods increased the pace of development of the factory and the city, especially in combination with the ever-expanding railways and allied means of transport and communication. The mass market was born, and workers increasingly became consumers.

New technologies demanded vast amounts of capital as well as large-scale organisation – hence the formation of joint-stock corporations often forming national and international cartels and trusts and using their strength to direct government policies on tariffs and trade unions, and even on foreign and colonial policy. Hence, too, the rise of a managerial and technocratic revolution, involving educated 'white collar workers' organising and planning the activities of skilled and unskilled 'blue collar workers'.

The agrarian way of life was still the most common, even in much of the more developed world, but was under threat, with the consequent danger of social dislocation. This would become an even greater likelihood if accompanied by unrest in the cities, which were beginning to predominate in the north and northwest of Europe, including Britain, and in parts of the USA.

Some factory workers were recent immigrants from the countryside; some were following the footsteps of their parents and grandparents. Equally, the bourgeoisie contained some families established in the class for several, even many generations, and others whose wealth or professional expertise was only recently acquired. Experience and attitudes could vary enormously within the wide frameworks of the class that owned property and the class that owned none. Women, especially from the upper and middle classes, often remained at home, supervising the activities of their domestic servants whose drudgery was at least a little relieved by the advent of labour-saving devices such as the sewing machine, and later the vacuum cleaner and washing machine. But many working-class women were employed for as many hours as their men-folk in the textile and other industries.

Generally speaking, the concerns of Malthus regarding overpopulation were largely ignored as the Second Industrial Revolution swallowed up men and women in its ever more greedy appetite for labour.

New History and Culture

Accurate mirrors of society before 1914 were provided by novelists depicting life in the encroaching city; composers catching the music of the disappearing rural society; painters inspired by the Second Industrial Revolution or apprehensive of its implications; and so on. Moreover, there was enough in common and indeed enough interaction between the various national cultures for contemporaries to talk more than

Burke at the end of the eighteenth century of a distinctively European culture, even of a Western culture combining the European with the American. However, the First World War and the Russian Revolution led to cultural disruption.

Before 1914, historians were attempting to analyse and synthesise the remote and recent past in a fresh manner. At the Congress of Arts and Science held along with the Universal Exposition in St Louis in 1904, the president of Princeton University and future president of the USA Woodrow Wilson welcomed 'the dawn...of a new age in the writing of history', in which 'no piece of history is true when set apart to itself, divorced and isolated'. He added, 'It is part of an intricately various whole, and must needs be put in its place in the netted scheme of events to receive its true color and estimation; and yet it must be itself individually studied and contrived if the whole is not to be weakened by its imperfection.' Two kinds of history, a 'record of experience' of events on the one hand and a 'record of evolution' of interpretation on the other could be combined as new kinds of enquiry were developed, including economic and social history. In this process, however, human experience must be kept separate from the story of nature, including geology, and even from animal life whose evolution was 'part of ours'. Of course, Wilson could not be aware that he was living in the Anthropocene Era, in which geology was merging with history. His outlook, therefore, was strictly anthropocentric.[7]

Wilson's views on the separation of human experience from the story of nature were no doubt shared by his colleagues, one of whom, James Harvey Robinson, argued that history could never become a science like chemistry or zoology. Rather, history would progress as a science with dependence on the development of cognate sciences such as 'politics, comparative jurisprudence, political economy, anthropology, sociology, perhaps above all of psychology'. Frederick Jackson Turner argued that 'the problems most important for consideration by historians of America are not those of the narrative of events or of the personality of the leaders, but rather those which arise when American history is viewed as the record of society in a wilderness environment'. Like Robinson, he argued that historians should draw on other academic disciplines as well as on literature and art. William M. Sloane included his fellow American George Bancroft along with the Englishman Macaulay and the German Ranke as the great historians of the nineteenth century, considering Bancroft 'their peer as scholar, philosopher, or statesman' and sharing Macaulay's 'insight and sympathy to catch the spirit of the age' in particular. Bancroft's profound conviction of God working in history and of democracy as the sole possibility for the realisation of human perfectibility was shared by many of his fellow Americans.[8]

Just a few years earlier, in the first volume of the *American Historical Review* published in 1896, Sloane had offered words of warning about too rapid a change. He observed: 'It seems to be the opinion of the keenest observers beyond the Atlantic that the old way today is weary of the past.' While Europe yearned for modernity and futurity, the tendency to move 'from experience towards theory, from adaptation towards experiment, from progress on traditional lines to advance on untried paths' was still 'in no sense characteristic of America'. But the easy circulation of ideas throughout the world might introduce that tendency into the USA, and Sloane had warned: 'if it comes or when it comes, and a conservative democracy guiding itself by the lights of history is transmuted into a radical ochlocracy moving by impulse or steering by wreckers' beacons, then, as it takes no prophetic gift to foretell, we shall have anarchy and ruin.' The 'radical ochlocracy' or proletariat was soon to make its impact in Europe, in Russia in 1917 in particular.[9]

In 1904, some historians from back across the Atlantic were among the participants at the Congress of Arts and Science in St Louis. One of them, Karl Lamprecht from Germany, advocated moving from specialisation towards universalism, from the 'individualist' approach to the 'collectivist', towards a scientific *Weltgeschichte* – world history. The greatest problem in this transition, Lamprecht asserted, was the deduction of a universal law from the history of the most important communities. Along with the USA and Japan these included the European countries that had undergone modernising experiences comparable to those in Germany. The study of some stages of development of 'over-ripe' or 'decadent' cultures such as the Indian or Chinese could be useful, but the centre of attention would have to be located where significant political and economic evolution had recently occurred. This, of course, Lamprecht conceded, was 'the doctrine of Karl Marx, the theory of the so-called, though most unhappily so-called, historical materialism'. However, in his view, the doctrine of Marx and his school was 'utterly inadequate' even if it were to include an attempt to measure the mental and moral progress of a community. Ethnology, archaeology and the history of art would all play important parts along with political and

economic history in the composition of *Weltgeschichte*. But, among all
the vast and inexhaustible sources of world history, the centre must be
emphatically 'psycho-historical'. Unfortunately, having set out the task,
Lamprecht came nowhere near completing it, partly because he could
not overcome the national sufficiently to approach the universal.[10]

Observing that the proclamation of the German Empire at
Versailles in 1871 was a great humiliation for France, Lamprecht
somewhat patronisingly conceded that, both in spite and because of
their revolutionary tradition, French intellectuals were managing
to make their own contribution to the development of the study of
history. Travellers perhaps more in the mind than in fact, the French
were not present at St Louis, but some of them shared the aspirations
of their colleagues. To take an outstanding example, having launched
the *Revue de Synthèse Historique* in 1900, Henri Berr published *La synthèse en
histoire: son rapport avec la synthèse générale* in 1911. In his view, the question
of scientific historical synthesis revolved around that of causality,
which consisted of three types or orders: contingency, necessity and
logic. Contingency involved not only chance but also six modes of
individuality: personal; 'collective'; geographical; through time; at any
moment; and (here Berr could not avoid using the German term) –
Völkerpsychologie – folk or national psychology, an area which Berr
believed to be an area much vaster and indeterminate than the word
itself might suggest, with a deep source expressing itself most clearly
in the various 'collective' individualities. If contingency in Berr's view
consisted of the facts, necessity was a matter of the social, and therefore
of sociology. The third order of causality, logic, meant for him ideas,
of psychology as well as sociology, which between them helped to bring
about the formation of consciousness (*conscience*). On the one hand,
Berr held back from asserting too rigid a system, a fault that he believed
he could find in sociology as developed by Emile Durkheim. On the
other hand, he was arguing against the establishment view of Charles
Seignobos, who recognised the necessity for selection and synthesis
as part of the process of document-based research, but also gave
emphasis to accidents, 'sudden crises caused by sudden events'. Berr
was to continue his ambitious but incomplete project after the First
World War, leading towards the creation by Marc Bloch and Lucien
Febvre of the journal *Annales* in 1929.[11]

The Italian Benedetto Croce, fluent but difficult to follow, argued
that 'true history is contemporary history', living again in the historian's

imagination, thus making the subject an art rather than a science.[12] Taking a different tack, the Russian V. O. Kliuchevsky observed:

> The law of the life of backward states or peoples among those which have outstripped it is that the need for reform arises earlier than the people is ready for reform. The necessity for movement in pursuit leads to the over-hasty adoption of the ways of others.

Kliuchevsky set out to present a 'historical sociology' of the many-sided activities of the peoples of the Russian Empire, but his experience of the revolution of 1905 led him to doubt that he could bring his account into the twentieth century. He also believed that national history should be seen as a part of a larger process, balancing internal against external pressures: only thus, for example, could it be understood why the Germans, as peaceful and friendly as any people in Europe at the beginning of the nineteenth century, had been transformed into aggressors who had advanced power as a principle of international relations.[13]

  Henri Berr was no doubt justified in his observation that Britain was far from adopting the objective scientific method in historical study, but continued to look upon the subject as a branch of general literature, against a strong background of the empiricist tradition. Nevertheless, the *Cambridge Modern History*, whose first volume was published in 1902, went some way towards adopting the approach of continental colleagues. It was arranged according to the plan of the late Lord Acton, who explained what he meant by 'Universal History':

> That which is distinct from the combined history of all countries, which is not a rope of sand, but a continuous development, and is not a burden on the memory, but an illumination of the soul. It moves in a succession to which the nations are subsidiary. Their story will be told, not for their own sake, but in reference and subordination to a higher series according to the time and degree in which they contribute to the common fortunes of mankind.

For Acton, 'the history of each people should be taken up at that point at which it was drawn into the main stream of human progress, as represented by the European nations'. Therefore, Russia did not emerge until Peter the Great, 'following the natural order of cause, not that of fortuitous juxtaposition'. The USA joined in at the date of its formation later in the eighteenth century, Acton succinctly making the point 'French Revolution – pathology, American – normal development of ideas': for him, the USA had produced 'a community more powerful, more prosperous, more intelligent and more free than any other the world has seen'.[14]

In 1903, Lord Acton's successor in the Regius Chair of Modern History at Cambridge, J. B. Bury, gave an inaugural lecture, 'The Science of History', in which he asserted that 'history is not a branch of literature' and that 'it has not yet become superfluous to insist that history is a science, no less and no more'. In 1904, at the Congress of Arts and Science in St Louis, he spoke on 'The Place of Modern History in the Perspective of Knowledge'. Noting that the invention of printing led to materials 'adequate for a complete analysis' and thus gave the modern period its theoretical significance, he went on to declare: 'it is the field in which we may hope to charm from human history the secret of its rational movement, detect its logic, and win a glimpse of a fragment of the pattern on a carpet, of which the greater part is still unwoven'. Expressed in a literary manner perhaps, but an aspiration towards science, nevertheless.[15]

In 1910, volume XII of the *Cambridge Modern History*, entitled 'The Latest Age', included Asia and Latin America to a much greater extent than hitherto, largely no doubt because, as the first sentence of its first chapter put it, 'In this period the History of Europe becomes in a sense the History of the world.' Later chapters demonstrated a new breadth not only in geographical coverage, but also in thematic approach, making reference to: the modern law of nations and the prevention of war, social movements, the scientific age, and the growth of 'historical science'. Concluding this last chapter, G. P. Gooch wrote: 'though the day may not yet have dawned when for working hypotheses shall be substituted a philosophy of history, defining and explaining the purpose and plan of human evolution, every true historian contributes, equally with the students of physical science and of psychology, to the progress of our knowledge of man'.[16]

A century later on, the day to which Gooch looked forward has still not dawned. Indeed, a prediction along comparable lines would appear more daring now than it did then, largely owing to discouraging human experiences and increasing complexities in natural and social sciences. Before the outbreak of the First World War, hopes such as those of

Gooch could be found throughout the Western world, although largely confined within a framework of varying national traditions.

Before 1914, the evolutionary, scientific approach enjoyed wide acceptance. Thus, the preface to the 11th edition of the *Encyclopaedia Britannica* in 1911 declared that it was 'dominated throughout by the historical point of view': that is, it attempted to consider a whole range of subjects 'in continual evolution…so that the salient facts might be included throughout, not merely as isolated events, but as part of a consistent whole, conceived in the spirit of the historian'. Statistics were used, and comparisons were made in the same spirit, while it was considered 'no less essential that the spirit of science should move over the construction of the work as a whole'. In order to achieve objectivity, contributors of all shades of opinion and of several different nationalities had cooperated, especially on controversial questions, and while individual judgements as to their relative claims might naturally vary, 'The general estimates which prevail among the countries which represent Western civilization are, however, in practical agreement on this point, and this consensus is the only ultimate criterion.' To take just one example, Max Weber was deemed to be the father of modern sociology, which was presented as 'the theory of organic evolution by natural selection' progressing along with the historical method through 'English utilitarianism…as influenced by the English theory of the rights of the individual on the one hand' and 'Marxian Socialism as influenced by the Latin conception of the omnipotence of the State on the other'. Marx himself was given four pages of exposition and analysis, while the major revisionist, Edouard Bernstein, who argued for the possibility of an evolutionary rather than revolutionary road to socialism, went unmentioned.

This neglect of important continental thinkers could be attributed partly to the circumstance that, although there were at least some continental contributors to the *Encyclopaedia Britannica*, its primary focus, like the majority of the contributors, was Anglo-American. However, the neglect could also result from the sheer impossibility of the assimilation of all features of a rapidly changing world in 'the spirit of science'. Could the encyclopaedia aiming at comprehensive coverage have passed its peak even before the onset of the First World War? In other languages, too, the heyday of the grand encyclopaedia was before 1914 – in French, German and Russian, in Spanish and Italian, Danish and Swedish, Polish and Czech, Hungarian and Romanian. In more recent times, however, it has been reborn in Wikipedia.

Throughout our discussion of culture, the emphasis has been on the high rather than the low. That is to say, we have neglected popular culture, whose more traditional aspects were under threat towards the end of the nineteenth century. Even before 1870, France and Prussia were well on their way to constructing a system of modern education; by 1914, virtually every European state had made arrangements for compulsory primary schooling. This remarkable spread of modern enlightenment did not take place without a struggle, not only against dark forces opposed to mass education of any kind but also between church and state, throughout continental Europe and even in Great Britain. This does not mean that churches refused to move with the times. For example, Pope Leo XIII made a spirited attempt to come to terms not only with the idea of popular education but also with socialism in such encyclicals as *Rerum novarum* (*Of New Matters*) in 1891.

One important consequence of the spread of literacy was the rise of the popular newspaper, leading to alarm in the ranks of the elite. With the Parisian *Le Petit Journal* reaching a circulation of 1 million by 1890, the historian Gabriel Monod lamented in 1898 that the French press was now 'little more than an agent of moral disintegration, a fomenter of hatred and of future civil wars'. In 1898, too, the influence of the Hearst press in the USA was widely believed to have contributed to the outbreak of the Spanish–American War. In the UK, the *Daily Mail* sold a million copies a day during the Boer War (1899–1902). In 1900, with the Boxer Rebellion in China in mind, the historian G. M. Trevelyan considered that the 'yellow peril' was less a threat to European civilisation than the 'white peril' consisting of 'the uniform modern man...creature of the great cities' moulded by 'the uprooting of taste and reason by the printing press'. The economist J. A. Hobson was moved to publish *The Psychology of Jingoism* in 1901, finding the 'chief engine' of the phenomenon in 'a biased, enslaved, and poisoned press'. At the end of the First World War, the philosopher Bertrand Russell considered that the press encouraging racism and nationalism had been one of the war's causes.[17] In the interwar period, the press would be even more 'biased, enslaved and poisoned', especially if not exclusively when taken over by extremist governments. Possibilities for influence and indoctrination increased with the spread of communication by radio before and during the Second World War – and by television and the internet afterwards.

The First World War and Russian Revolution

Both the First World War and the Russian Revolution arose from the imperial struggle for the 'survival of the fittest'. As with previous great events in history, however, there is no need to retell a familiar story here.

Before the beginning of hostilities in 1914, no crowned or even uncrowned head of state could be completely confident of his position. From one end of Europe to the other, there were pockets of unrest in town and country alike, partly caused perhaps by the preoccupation of governments with the international crisis but partly also as the result of the process of industrial modernisation. Perhaps the process was nearest to completion in Britain, although even there 1914 brought strikes of formidable proportions. In Russia, there was a widespread sense of living 'on a volcano' early in 1914, but historians are divided about the likelihood of revolution without war.[18]

At the outset of hostilities, however, social stability returned; there were great demonstrations in London and other capitals but these were not in favour of international brotherhood and the advancement of the cause of the working class. On the contrary, nearly everybody was swept up in a huge wave of patriotism and a backwash of xenophobia (a word for hatred of foreigners appropriately coined at about this time). The Almighty was called upon to intercede on behalf of the just cause by the clergy of all the warring nations, and believing that God as well as their own united people were on their side, millions of young men went off to do their bit, never to return. Thus society at all levels was deprived of the longer-term services of many of the most vigorous male members of a whole generation. Meanwhile, women did much more than weep and keep home fires burning, putting their shoulders to the wheels of industry as a practical example of the need for their emancipation.

Before 1914, the vast majority of workers belonged to no economic or political organisation. However, the threat to skilled workers from the influx of new, at best semiskilled workers necessitated by the onset of the Second Industrial Revolution grew with the need to produce the materials of war, leading to an increase of trade union membership, and to more confrontation with management. Political parties were formed or adapted themselves to respond to the aspirations of the proletariat.

Far from solving the problems of Europe, the First World War made them greater. The principal loser, Germany, was pushed into deep resentment; the chief European victors Britain and France were considerably weakened. The great powers that gained by far the most were outside Europe – especially the USA, and to some extent Japan. China began to assert its sovereignty, and the first intimations of independence were felt among many subject peoples throughout the world. As far as human war losses were concerned, American dead reached a total of about 100,000, while the British approached 1 million, the French and Austro-Hungarian exceeded it and the Russian and German numbers were both nearer to 2 millions. Well over 20 million civilians died in the years of the war and those immediately following, many of them in an epidemic of influenza. Having been largely ignored throughout the nineteenth century, the warnings of Malthus on overpopulation were pushed further into the background.

One of the major performers in the first act of the great Russian drama of revolution in 1917, the historian Paul Miliukov, observed in 1921 that

> just as a powerful geological cataclysm jokingly throws down the crust of the latest cultural strata and brings to the surface long-hidden seams recalling hoary antiquity – the remote epochs of the earth's history, so the Russian Revolution laid bare for us all our historical structure, only superficially covered by the thin layers of recent cultural acquisitions.[19]

Indeed, it was not just the politicians who were putting tsarism to the test. Even among the peasants, who were remote from the latest news and rumours, suspicion was growing of the 'little father', and a simple belief as ancient as the folk wisdom was again coming to the surface: the land was theirs. And while the vast majority of the Russian people in the provinces were beginning to agitate for their rights, that small but significant minority in Petrograd (as the capital city had been renamed to avoid the Germanic 'Sankt Peterburg') and other cities were already more active in pursuit of justice for the workers. A third category of dissidence was to be found among the non-Russian nationalities, showing their dissatisfaction with their recent treatment in the empire, even though their incorporation had sometimes occurred centuries ago. Questions surrounding the peasants, workers and nationalities, as well as unrest among the soldiers and sailors confronted Lenin and the Bolsheviks after their seizure of power in October 1917, just as they had faced Kerensky and the Provisional Government following the overthrow of tsarism in February.

The Circumstances of Peace

The major European imperial powers had become exhausted in the struggle among themselves, bringing the period of European world dominance closer to its end. The greatest world power from 1918 onwards was the USA, which had moved during the Second Industrial Revolution to first position in economic strength, a position confirmed at the end of the First World War by its assumption of leadership in financial affairs. These basic facts were real enough, although disguised in the short run by the more dramatic nature of the Russian Revolution and by the USA's retreat towards isolation. The USA's full emergence as a superpower would not take place until after the Second World War. Meanwhile, by external force and by internal inclination, the Soviet Union had been cut off from Europe. Some years later than the USA, it too emerged after the Second World War as a superpower.

Back in 1919, the Soviet threat was in the minds of the statesmen working on the Treaty of Versailles and other agreements after the First World War was over, but the Russian Revolution was incomplete. Versailles and other treaties stemming from the Paris Peace Conference weakened Germany but did not dismember it, as a *cordon sanitaire* against Bolshevism was set up in Eastern Europe. For two global visions confronted each other: on the one hand, there was Wilson's liberal belief in a world made safe for democracy; on the other hand, Lenin's Marxist belief in world proletarian revolution. The American president wanted the League of Nations to arrange the affairs of mankind, the Soviet leader aimed at the influence of the Third (Communist) International. Wilson was devoted to the Open Door and the freedom of economic activity everywhere. Lenin asserted that capitalism had reached the highest stage of its activity, imperialism, and was on the brink of collapse, to be succeeded by socialism, for him a system in which the dictatorship of the proletariat would bring to an end the exploitation of the workers by the capitalists.

Conclusion

During the period 1871–1921, Dame Nature had given powerful reminders that humankind was not solely responsible for the world's disasters. There was a huge eruption at Krakatoa in the South Seas in 1883, and a reminder in Europe of the power of the volcano from Vesuvius in 1906. In 1908, a meteorite exploded over a remote part of Siberia making a huge blast field. As already noted, a global flu pandemic broke out at the end of the First World War. On the other hand, natural phenomena could have a benign influence: in November 1919, photographs of an eclipse of the sun verified the concept of relativity that Einstein had begun to advance in 1905. Einstein entered popular consciousness as the scientist par excellence.

Two outstanding individuals answering to the political demands of the time were Woodrow Wilson and Vladimir Lenin. Both of them were prolific authors as well as outstanding statesmen. Thus, their contemporaries in the USA and the USSR as well as wider afield were soon ready to attribute great significance to them. Already in October 1918, for example, the German-born Swiss essayist and playwright Herman Kesser wrote: 'It is certain that mankind must make up its mind either for Wilson or for Lenin.'[20] Today, with the advantages of hindsight, we may perhaps be permitted to argue that they were both products of a dual process of natural selection. That is to say, they rose to their positions of prominence by acting on their keen understanding of the opportunities for influence over the masses afforded by the circumstances in which they found themselves.

These would include the special position of their two countries in the global imperial rivalry, the USA as a vigorous newcomer, tsarist Russia as a tiring veteran. The USA was a leader in the Second Industrial Revolution, while Russia was, comparatively speaking and for most of the time, finding it difficult to keep up. Much the same could be said about their rates of cultural advance.

In the future, the struggle between Wilsonism and Leninism would have a profound effect on the writing of history. In the period leading up to the First World War, there were some signs of the subject undergoing, like industry and natural science, a kind of revolution, opening itself up to the influence of other disciplines and aspiring to a new universality. However, with the confrontation between Wilsonism and Leninism, even more with the arrival of Italian Fascism and German Nazism, hopes for further advances in common historical understanding were to be dashed.

Chapter 5

FROM RELATIVITY TO TOTALITARIANISM, 1921–1945

After the photographs taken of a solar eclipse verified Einstein's theory of relativity in 1919, articles on the subject immediately began to appear in the *Times* of London, the *New York Times* and other newspapers. Books discussing relativity by Arthur Eddington, James Jeans and Bertrand Russell soon entered the best-seller lists. Einstein himself deplored the application of the term in other branches of enquiry, including history, and to the human experience in general. However, J. D. Bernal aptly commented in 1969 that

> the effect of Einstein's work, outside the narrow specialist fields where it can be applied, was one of general mystification. It was eagerly seized on by the disillusioned intellectuals after the First World War to help them in refusing to face realities. They only needed to use the word 'relativity' and say 'Everything is relative', or 'It depends on what you mean'. Relativity formed the basis of the work of many popularizations of the mysteries of science.[1]

Here, we will go with the popular flow, as we apply the term to developments from 1921 to 1939 in general. Undoubtedly, European 'disillusioned intellectuals' could no longer accept the coherence of Europe as accepted by Gibbon and Burke in the eighteenth century and others since, while their American counterparts of the 'lost generation' no longer possessed their prewar certainties either.

'Normalcy' and Breakdown, 1921–1929

In his first message to Congress, delivered in person on 12 April 1921, President Warren G. Harding called for a return to 'normalcy'.

At home, this meant reduction of expenditure and taxation, and of government interference in general. Abroad, this would mean the rejection of the League of Nations. However, Harding declared, 'we make no surrender of our hope and aim for an association to promote peace, in which we would most heartily join'.[2] For this purpose, in particular, the president would soon sign treaties with Germany and other former enemies. To former allies, he sent out invitations in July 1921 to an international conference to convene in November in Washington DC on the limitation of armaments.

At the opening of the Washington Conference in November 1921, Charles Evans Hughes, the secretary of state, shocked the delegates (especially the British, who had become accustomed to ruling the waves) with a proposal for the introduction of a 5:5:3 ratio for the capital ships of the major navies, the British, the American and the Japanese. Not because of his eloquence, but because the First World War had made his country the world's greatest power, Hughes was also able to bring to an end the Anglo–Japanese Alliance established in 1902, and to assert the 'Open Door' principle of international law for application in China in particular. Thus was formed the Versailles–Washington system of international relations, together attending to the strategic priorities on land and at sea set out previously by Mackinder and Mahan.

Back in Europe, a conference assembled in Genoa in the spring of 1922 to discuss the renewal of relations between Soviet Russia and the other European states, along with some non-European (although the USA declined an invitation). The principal outcome was indirect and unwelcome to the former Allies: the signing on 6 April at nearby Rapallo of a separate treaty by the two major powers kept out of the postwar peace negotiations and the League of Nations, Soviet Russia and Weimar Germany. Dealing mainly with diplomatic recognition and economic readjustment, they laid the foundations for mutually advantageous recovery. Thus, the Versailles–Washington system was fragile from the start.

As for the League of Nations, although Germany became a member in 1926 and joined Britain, France, Italy and Japan as a permanent member of the council, the USA continued to remain aloof and the USSR was still excluded. However, in 1927 the USA responded positively to an overture from the French foreign minister, Aristide Briand, suggesting their mutual renunciation of war; indeed, Secretary of State Frank B. Kellogg proposed that all nations be invited to join in. Several of them accepted the invitation in August 1928 when the Kellogg–Briand Pact or Pact of Paris was drawn up, condemning and renouncing recourse to war as an instrument of national policy or a solution of international dispute. Quite soon, no fewer than 65 states including the USSR had agreed to outlaw war. As in earlier agreements, the USA insisted that the Monroe Doctrine concerning the Americas would have to be observed and Britain made a similar reservation concerning the security of the British Empire.

Generally speaking, before the Depression, the 1920s were coming to an end with high hopes for the preservation of peace. On the whole, however, the 1920s were not good years for democracy. Taking advantage of some of the errors made in the war and insults allegedly handed out in the immediate peace, Mussolini rose to power in Italy after a march on Rome in 1922. His Fascist government soon eliminated vestiges of political opposition. According to the new leader, 'The Doctrine of Fascism'

> is opposed to classical Liberalism, which arose from the necessity of reacting against absolutism, and which brought its historical purpose to an end when the State was transformed into the conscience and will of the people... Outside the State there can be neither individuals nor groups... Therefore Fascism is opposed to Socialism, which confines the movement of history within the class struggle and ignores the unity of classes established in one economic and moral reality in the State... Fascism is opposed to Democracy, which equates the nation to the majority... Fascism desires the State to be strong, organic and at the same time founded on a wide popular basis.[3]

Agreement with Mussolini's authoritarian methods if not necessarily with all his ideas spread throughout many countries of Europe, for example Spain and Portugal, Poland and Hungary, Romania, Bulgaria and Yugoslavia . Most threatening of all developments for many observers were to be seen not on the Right but on the Left, in the Union of Soviet Socialist Republics, set up officially in December 1922. As Stalin's hold over the USSR became stronger after the death of Lenin early in 1924, apprehension about the nature of the Soviet Union became keener, especially towards the end of the decade. The 'normalcy' of which President Harding had spoken was turning out to be a strange phenomenon indeed.

Discussion of the Depression of 1929 and succeeding years is sometimes set against a background assumption that the norm for most people in the industrialising world had always been prosperity. In fact, the reverse was nearer the case, even in those periods when the panics, crashes and slumps of earlier years had been overcome. Still the basic problem remained the same, the maldistribution of wealth, too few rich and too many poor. As ever, if the whole world were included in the discussion, the gap would appear even wider, the imbalance even greater. There were some special features to the situation in 1929, nevertheless, most of which arose from the First World War and its immediate aftermath. The great conflict had accelerated the emergence of the USA as the world's leading financial power while the major states of Europe had spent their treasure in the attempt to blow each other to bits. American loans went to all the major belligerents, and more were extended after the Armistice of 1918. The problem then became compounded as the passionate desire to make Germany pay led to the imposition of reparations that Germany soon found it impossible to keep up with, and so once again the dollar had to step in. A vicious financial triangle arose, as the USA lent money to Germany to make its reparations to Britain and France so that they in turn could send at least some of the money they owed back to the USA. The impact of the Great Depression was worldwide, for example in Japan as well as in the USA and Europe.

The Revival of History

World war and revolution struck a great blow at Europe in particular. Perhaps no other book caught the spirit of the immediately following times as Oswald Spengler's *Der Untergang des Abendland* translated as *The Decline of the West*. In an article of 1919, Spengler wrote: 'The nineteenth century was the century of natural science; the twentieth belongs to psychology. We no longer believe in the power of reason over life. We feel that life governs reason.' In *The Decline of the West*, published in full in 1922 and 1923, Spengler declared that the historian must become a relativist and realise that 'his "unshakable" truths and "eternal" views are simply true for him and eternal for his world-view'.[4] He rejected the traditional chronological exposition of human evolution from ancient to modern times in favour of a comparative study of civilisations or cultures, in particular of classical Greece and Rome with the contemporary West, with some reference to others. He put forward a pessimistic cyclical interpretation of history, rejecting ideas of progress, democracy and world peace. On the other hand, G. M. Trevelyan wrote mostly on the narrative of England's past in fine confident style, rejecting French as well as German approaches and insisting that its prime purpose was to educate Englishmen. 'We must be ourselves', he declared, observing in 1919 that 'Englishmen need no longer apologise for the free traditions of their own history and of their own great national historians', especially 'seeing what a dance German "scientific" history has led the nation that looked to it for political prophecy and guidance'.[5]

In 1921, the American historian Charles A. Beard set off to see for himself the predicament of Europe. Having resigned from Columbia University in 1917 in solidarity with two colleagues dismissed for opposing the war policies of Woodrow Wilson, Beard tried to find out how much of Warren Harding's 'normalcy' could be found in the continent that had borne the brunt of the war's hostilities. On his return, he gave a series of lectures at Dartmouth College, published in 1922 under the title *Crosscurrents in Europe Today*. Beard described his book as 'a collection of notes' which he hoped would be pertinent 'to the great case of Mankind vs. Chaos'. Looking at that part of Europe where chaos appeared to be posing the greatest threat in the shape of the Russian Revolution, he suggested that Lenin had never been deceived by 'the childish phantasy that paper decrees would establish the new heaven and the new earth' and had demonstrated since the October Revolution 'the doctrine of the pragmatist'. In 1922, with the New Economic Policy often described as a compromise with the peasant majority under way, it seemed to Beard 'fairly safe to guess' that Russia would evolve into 'a huge peasant democracy' and that 'a form of state capitalism' would take 'the place of communism'. Throughout the continent, the American historian believed, socialists had put 'Marx on the shelf' and taken a course in efficiency management, having realised that 'rhetoric does not build names' and 'party programs do not make plows'. As for that other great force, nationalism, Beard hoped that statesmen would come to see that its ethnic and geographical bases had nothing to do with prosperity, and that 'some kind of a general economic constitution' would be adopted throughout the continent.

Meanwhile, the 'new America' would be forced by the 'paralysis of Europe' to look upon the Pacific region as 'the new theatre'.[6]

In 1922 in revolutionary Russia, E. V. Tarle addressed the problems facing the study of history in an article entitled 'The Next Task'. He identified three in particular: the overwhelming number of facts coming from the archives; the growth of new disciplines, especially economic history; and the broadening of horizons, in particular through the increasing complications of psychology. 'Revolution is always first and foremost death, then life', Tarle observed, but warned of the dangers of historians being diverted from their main purpose by 'loss of faith in the correctness of a whole range of their former convictions', 'new and powerful temptations', and 'powerful, often uncertain influences'. Revolution made nervous people believe that they were becoming delirious. On the contrary, believing that they were in 'an unbreakable and majestic ark...they were previously delirious, lulled by a false security, forgetting that not far under the elegant carpet of their cabin there is a dark and fathomless abyss'. Only through a combination of scholarship and synthesis could progress be made, Tarle argued, emphasising that 'The more powerful, the more *authentic* the generalising thought, the more it needs the erudite and erudition.'[7] A different, more orthodox point of view was put forward throughout the 1920s by M. N. Pokrovsky, who defined his approach as 'politics projected into the past' and reduced Russia before the Revolution to a somewhat schematic arena for the class struggle devoid of individual personality. In his *Brief History of Russia* (1931), moreover, he asserted that 'It is easy to foresee that in the future, when science and technique have attained to perfection which we are as yet unable to visualise, nature will become soft wax in his [man's] hands which he will be able to cast into whatever form he chooses.'[8]

Back in the spring of 1923, ten years almost to the day after its predecessor in London, the much-delayed Fifth Congress of Historical Sciences met in Brussels. A keynote address was given by a leading Belgian historian Henri Pirenne, who had no doubt been given the opportunity for much reflection in a prisoner-of-war camp, as well as writing a history of Europe from memory.[9] Taking as his theme 'On the Comparative Method in History', Pirenne began with earlier, happier memories of the prewar meeting in London, in particular the appeal of Lord Bryce for international agreement based on historical solidarity. He recalled, too, how the decision had been taken in London for the next congress to meet in St Petersburg. Alas, by 1917, civilisation was undergoing the most terrible crisis ever, and all energies were being devoted to its resolution. St Petersburg had become Petrograd, and the Russian Revolution as well as the world war made a congress there impossible. Peace had ensued, Pirenne continued, but had given the world neither security nor serenity. How many problems still had to be solved, he exclaimed, and how much moral and intellectual disarray could be observed, along with the disturbance of the social and economic equilibrium. In spite of all these and other difficulties, historians had resumed their pursuit of truth with as much detachment as possible, in the spirit of Louis Pasteur, who had observed: 'It is a question of fact, and I approach it without any preconceived idea. I can only yield to experience, whatever the answer.' And now, among these facts were all those accumulated during the war, which had in general enlarged the nature of the subject.

During the war, the belligerents had requisitioned for their own use two sciences in particular – chemistry and history. One had provided explosives[10] and gas, the other pretexts, justifications and excuses. But their fate had differed: chemistry could serve armies and preserve its nature, even make precious discoveries, while history lost its essential qualities of criticism and impartiality. This loss could always be found in time of war, since to interpret princely genealogies and discuss treaties as under the Ancien Régime was no longer enough: now the morale of one's own people had to be maintained by, among other methods, academic attacks on the enemy. However, such work had served only to demonstrate the lack of a scientific basis for the excesses of nationalism – for racial theories. There was no such phenomenon as pure race, and various peoples had developed at different rates not because of racial characteristics but because of different circumstances. This meant that at any given time the peoples of the world belonged to various stages of development. Nevertheless, they all went through comparable stages, and the only way to understand their individuality was to compare their experiences. Only in such a manner was it possible to achieve scientific knowledge.

This was a demanding task, and the objection would be raised that it was beyond any single individual historian; no chemist could know all chemistry, still less all nature. Specialisation was therefore as necessary in chemistry as in history, but in both from a point of view that was universal. The universal approach to history had been established up to and during the eighteenth century, but Romanticism and nationalism had introduced diversity in the nineteenth century. This was far from being an entirely backward step, since the search for local colour and differences between peoples had made history more lively, picturesque and thrilling than it had ever been, just at the same time as the criticism of sources and enquiry into all branches of social activity – law, customs and economy, for example – had made the subject richer and more precise. Deservedly, the nineteenth should be called the century of history.

However, this achievement must be considered scholarly rather than scientific. Apparently, as the field of history widened, its vision became narrower, ever shrinking as it approached the present, that is as nationalism and imperialism asserted themselves and produced an exclusiveness in the approach to the past. The consequent lack of impartiality might be unwitting, but it was certainly fatal:

> The prejudices of race, politics and nationalism are too powerful for man to escape if he does not place himself outside their grasp. To liberate oneself, it is necessary to raise oneself to the heights from which history appears as a whole in the majesty of its development, the passing passions of the moment become calm and subside before the sublimity of the spectacle.

Pirenne claimed no originality for his own views, and saluted the manner in which others had put them forward before the war. One of these, Henri Berr, for example, was still active, now engaged in a great project begun in 1920 with the title 'The Evolution of Humanity'. But Pirenne believed it necessary to emphasise that the only way of arriving at the desired destination was via the comparative method. That was the only way to allow history to free itself from the idols of sentiment and become a science. History would also become a science to the extent that it adopted for national history the point of view of universal history. And as it did so, it would become not only more exact but also more humane: 'The scientific will go hand in hand with the moral gain, and nobody will complain if it should one day inspire in peoples, through showing them the solidarity of their destinies, a patriotism more fraternal, more aware (*conscient*) and more pure.'

Unfortunately, even tragically, as is well known, the hopes held out by Pirenne were being dashed almost as he spoke. Indeed, it could be argued that the impact of the First World War, the Russian Revolutions and their aftermaths was such that his address was a vain appeal for historians to meet an impossible standard. Certainly, Pirenne appears to have surmounted the effect of his own harrowing experiences, and could therefore be forgiven for daring to suggest that others might follow suit. Several historians indeed did, but the sequel was not just a matter of personal choice, and some brave souls were overwhelmed during the interwar years and the Second World War.

Pirenne himself not only completed a multivolumed history of Belgium but also endeavoured to look outwards. For example, just before his death in 1935, he completed a draft of a study of the relationship between two great figures of the early Middle Ages, arguing that Charlemagne would not have developed as he did without Mahomet. Soon after his death, his son published the history of Europe from the end of the Roman Empire to the sixteenth century, all that his father had been able to complete while interned during the First World War of a work planned to reach 1914. Pirenne enjoyed a close relationship with Marc Bloch and other leading figures of the French *Annales* school. Stemming in some ways from the 'synthesis' movement initiated by Henri Berr in 1900, the *Annales* school did as much as any other group during the interwar period to point the way forward, struggling to overcome the restrictions of tradition and nationality.[11] As we shall see, *Annales* was almost alone.

From Depression to War, 1929–1939, and History

In Europe, the Depression brought harsh remedies for severe problems, especially in Germany, and even more, if less directly, in the Soviet Union. Like the Fascists under Mussolini in Italy, the Nazis under Hitler had borrowed some of the Left's ideas to gain followers among the lower orders of society on behalf of the Right. There were nevertheless some important elements in their appeal and success that came from inside German traditions. These included vague and even artificial memories of a golden age, whether in the nineteenth century at the time of the Second Reich or back as far as the ninth century and the First Reich of Charlemagne or Charles the Great, even stretching back to a prehistorical folk past. Then, there was the love of ceremonial – flags, uniforms and parades – involving above all the heroic leader embodying nationalist aspirations and the purity of the race. Moreover,

the rapid pace of Germany's modernisation process in the fifty years
or so before 1914, as well as the joys and agonies of the war period,
1914–18, gave the emotions of its superficially stolid people both
intensity and instability. None of this, however, would have become
as explicit and dominant without the economic crisis, which brought
Hitler's movement the support of many great landowners and of some
big businessmen, especially from the coal and iron industries, and of
the generals.

Meanwhile, as what Hitler called the fight against 'Jewish-Bolshevik'
world conspiracy[12] was being prepared, there was no lack of awareness
of the approaching attack in the principal target for his denunciations
and diatribes, the Soviet Union. However, if German autarky was a
deliberate policy, Soviet autarky was largely enforced and added to the
relentless pace of the Five-Year Plans accompanied by Stalin's purges.

In the 1930s, Europe's place in the world was indeed less
prominent than it had been a half-century or so previously, partly
because of the rise to world power of the USA and Japan. Generally
speaking, the outlook of European statesmen had not adapted to
such changing times: they did not see sufficiently clearly that the
1930s were not pre-1914.

As Italy and Germany succumbed to dictatorship, extremely
nationalistic history became established, and historians such as Croce
and Meinecke were forced to conform or compromise, remain silent
or go into exile. No branch of Nazi historiography was as warped as
that dealing with Eastern Europe, the land promised by the Führer as
Lebensraum for the *Herrenvolk* after the elimination of Jewish and Slavonic
Untermenschen. Although some scholars in Eastern Europe resisted the
urge to respond in kind, intense nationalism of both right-wing and
left-wing varieties developed there too, even in the alleged home of
class-based internationalism, the USSR. Across the Atlantic, Europe's
other outlier, the USA, could not escape some of the intellectual and
anti-intellectual waves sweeping over the ocean.

Across the Channel, like G. M. Trevelyan, H. A. L. Fisher had no
faith in history as science, declaring in 1936:

> Men wiser and more learned than I have discerned in history a
> plot, a rhythm, a predetermined pattern. These harmonies are
> concealed from me. I can see only one emergency following upon
> another as wave follows upon wave, only one great fact with respect

to which, since it is unique, there can be no generalizations, only one safe rule for the historian: that he should recognize in the development of human destinies the play of the contingent and the unforeseen. This is not a doctrine of cynicism and despair. The fact of progress is written plain and large on the page of history; but progress is not a law of nature. The ground gained by one generation may be lost by the next. The thoughts of men may flow into the channels which lead to disaster and barbarism.

Fisher described the history of Europe from Greece onwards, beginning with the assertion that 'We Europeans are the children of Hellas.' Nevertheless, he acknowledged the importance of the first and second industrial revolutions as embodied in steam and electricity, adding: 'It is possible that two thousand years hence these two scientific inventions may be regarded as constituting the "Great Divide" in human history.'[13]

As an example of developments in the USSR, let us follow the career of E. V. Tarle. During the 1920s, he was able to coexist with his Marxist colleagues, although he was attacked as a 'pseudo-Marxist' in 1928. He was criticised in particular for denying the intensification of the class struggle during the years 1872–1914, and exaggerating the responsibility of Germany in particular rather than the Western powers in general for the First World War. In 1930, he was arrested, implicated in a 'plot' to restore tsarism and sent into exile. However, in 1934, Tarle was rehabilitated, and resumed his career for a further twenty years or so, collecting honours on the way. He wrote patriotic works on the war against Napoleon and the Crimean War among many others, taking care to avoid the repetition of earlier errors. Meanwhile, Pokrovsky, who had dominated Soviet historiography throughout the 1920s with heavy emphasis on the class struggle, was disestablished, and great efforts were made to produce textbooks appropriate for the context of the Five-Year Plans, reverting to patriotic narrative.

In the USA, Charles A. Beard changed historical tack after the Great Depression. In his presidential address to the American Historical Association, 'Written History as an Act of Faith', delivered at the end of 1933, he declared: 'Having broken the tyranny of physics and biology, contemporary thought in historiography turns its engines of verification upon the formula of historical relativity – the formula that makes all written history merely relative to time and circumstance, a passing shadow, an illusion.'

In furtherance of his preoccupation, Beard developed an interest in the German Friedrich Meinecke's *historismus*, an argument for 'the replacement of the generalizing view of historico-human forces by an individualizing view', including the recognition that 'each time... has its own style'. However, in 1937, along with Alfred Vagts, Beard dubbed Meinecke 'the historian of State Reason' and criticised him for not making a clear distinction between the conditions in which German, French, British and American thought evolved. All historians, they argued, recognised that it was impossible to know history as it had actually been and would develop a 'scheme of reference', liberal, fascist, Marxist or other. But there was now wide agreement that their province should include some aspects of biological enquiry, for example 'biometric investigations of genius, character and family traits'. All historians, Beard and Vagts concluded, whatever their speciality, had 'a public responsibility: the kind of history they write, whether good or bad, helps to make history in spite of their efforts to escape from the outcome of their own labors'.[14]

The Second World War, 1939–1945, and History

There is no need here to tell the story of the Second World War, nor to describe the patriotic effusions of historians at any length. To take the example of the USA, Peter Novick writes:

> The aftermath of World War I ushered in a period of negativity and doubt, the climate in which the relativist critique flourished. The coming of World War II saw American culture turn toward affirmation and the search for certainty. American mobilization, intellectual as well as material, became permanent in what most saw as one continuous struggle of the 'Free World' against 'totalitarianism' – first in its Nazi, then its Soviet embodiments.

Novick also suggests that the Soviet historian E. V. Tarle wrote 'in terms which were virtually identical to those being used in the United States'.[15] G. M. Trevelyan and Herbert Butterfield were among those flying the flag in the United Kingdom. There is even less need to consider what

Beard and Vogts called the 'scheme of reference' for the racist, hateful kind of history being put out in Germany, Italy and Japan.

Instead of following patriotic and xenophobic effusions further, let us return to the significant question of the role of the individual, even if falling short of the suggestion of Beard and Vogts that historians might contribute in some way to 'biometric investigations of genius, character and family traits'. Like Napoleon, Bismarck, Lenin and Wilson before them, a number of men (they were all men) were considered to have played an outstanding part in history, on this occasion to have caused the war or to have won it. Leaving aside Hitler, Mussolini, Tojo and the other 'villains', let us turn to the 'heroes', the five individuals successively constituting the 'Big Three' whose meetings have often been considered to have made a major contribution to the ultimate triumph of the anti-Axis coalition: Churchill, Roosevelt and Stalin, then Truman and Attlee. A tentative conclusion could be that they all had their 'great' moments in history. Churchill's finest hour was the earlier years of the Second World War. Roosevelt's New Deal already qualified him for greatness before his drive and his vision from Pearl Harbor to his death. Bad man though he is widely agreed to have been, Stalin demonstrated determined leadership in the Great Patriotic War. Truman and Attlee had their greatness thrust upon them with their unexpected appearance at the last Big Three conference at Potsdam in 1945, the former taking the USA into cold war 'superpowerdom', the latter reconciling Great Britain to the beginning of the process of decolonisation.

However, the five individuals appear to have thought that they had a greater influence over the course of events than seems to be the case in retrospect. We may approach this observation counterfactually, and in various ways. At the most basic level, had the Channel not existed, Churchill could not have been a great war leader; nor could Stalin had there been no vast Russian plain. Without the USA's long preparation for 'superpowerdom' in the secure Western hemisphere, Roosevelt could not have stood out as he did. Truman would not have been so assertive with no atom bomb, nor Attlee had the end of empire not pressed so heavily upon him.

Let us recall that all five members of the Big Three were creatures of the nineteenth century, imbued – albeit in different ways – with the idea of progress and the concept of the 'great man'. (As in so many other respects, Stalin was an exception, but his avowed creed Marxism shared the basic supposition of progress, while in his official view there was no greater hero than Lenin.) No doubt, their strong will was a consequence of the common beliefs of their time, sustaining them all through severe illness (with the exception of Truman – the only non-smoker among them, incidentally – who appears to have enjoyed mostly good health, leaving high office in 1953 in a better condition than when he entered it in 1945) and the approach of death. But, to take just one counterfactual example, what if Stalin had died instead of Roosevelt in April 1945? Subsequent events might have turned out better with the departure of a dictator, they could have been worse in the panic that would have ensued in the struggle for the succession.[16]

No doubt, the Big Three were also sustained by the high degree of public confidence that they enjoyed during the Second World War and just after. Had they been in office at a less critical time, they might have been given less subsequent attention. To take one example, Churchill was in the political wilderness before his recall to high office in 1940, and would not otherwise have been considered to be the embodiment of the British 'Bulldog' spirit. And evaluation might have been less positive had they been more exposed to the media. Let us recall that the press had limited access to the deliberations of the Big Three, radio and newsreel even less, television – none. It is difficult to imagine them all emerging unscathed from rigorous interviews.

A final question needs to be posed, were the various members of the Big Three indeed 'great men'? Unfortunately or luckily, depending on how you look at it, there can be no final answer. While psychologists have no certain explanation of the workings of the human brain, there can be no completely satisfying explanation of the thoughts of political leaders, let alone their interaction with those of their followers. However, some of us will want to agree with Carlyle, Plekhanov and Braudel that the truly great men are those who direct the tide a little at least as they swim with it. The individuals who believed that they were in a position to solve the world's problems in 1945 all deserve inclusion in the top rank. Undoubtedly, as their discussions at Tehran, Yalta and Potsdam demonstrated, together they helped to win the Second World War even if their disagreements pointed towards an uneasy peace.

Beyond the Big Three, there were millions making heroic sacrifices or simply unfortunate enough to be in the wrong place at the wrong time. The greatest losses were those of the Soviet Union, at least 20 and possibly more than 40 million, and of China, an even more difficult number to determine, but probably more than 15 million. Then, in approximate millions, come Poland – 6, Germany – 5, Japan – 2, Yugoslavia – 1.5, France – 0.6, the United Kingdom – 0.4 and the USA – 0.3. Civilian deaths were more numerous than the military, most notoriously the Jews murdered in the Holocaust – up to 6 million, and millions more Slav '*Untermenschen*' and Chinese were exterminated too. Citizens of Hiroshima and Nagasaki were the first to be eliminated by a new form of weapon – the atomic bomb. In such circumstances, to talk like Malthus about the dangers of overpopulation would have seemed obscene.

The Arrival of the Atomic Bomb

During the years 1921–1945, as the implications of the theories of Einstein and his contemporaries were more widely realised, the individual scientist could no longer operate alone, and had to depend on others. Institutional, often governmental, support was necessary. Meanwhile, the interaction of the sciences was taken to a new level, and the whole process of advance accelerated. Let us recall how long it took for Watt's steam engine to be adapted for the purposes of locomotion. Let us recall, too, how evaluations of the nineteenth century at the beginning of the twentieth had remarked on the increased pace of change. Obviously, they had seen nothing yet.

From the point of view of 1945, the most significant discoveries were in physics, leading to the atom bomb. They resembled the development of the steam engine only in the necessity of networking for the completion of the task. In 1939, an ominous year for other reasons, Albert Einstein was prompted to write to President Roosevelt on 2 August, setting out the problem and giving due recognition to some of the individuals concerned:

In the course of the last four months it has been made probable – through the work of Joliot in France as well as Fermi and Szilard in America – that it may become possible to set up a nuclear chain reaction in a large mass of uranium, by which vast amounts of power and large quantities of new radium-like elements would be generated. Now it appears almost certain that this could be achieved in the immediate future.

This new phenomenon would also lead to the construction of bombs, and it is conceivable – though much less certain – that extremcly powerful bombs of a new type may thus be constructed…. In view of this situation you may think it desirable to have some permanent contact maintained between the Administration and the group of physicists working on chain reactions in America.[17]

But Einstein, the best-known theoretician of the twentieth century, was not to be involved directly in the making of the atomic bomb.

The development of the A-bomb involved a considerable number of individuals and groups in various places: for example Cambridge and Copenhagen as well as Los Alamos and Oak Ridge. Of the three men mentioned by Einstein in his letter to Roosevelt, Frédéric Joliot collaborated in Paris with his wife Irène, the daughter of Marie Curie, primarily in radioactivity research; Enrico Fermi discovered the 'neutrino' and much else in Rome en route before further work on nuclear fission in New York; and Leo Szilard, an itinerant Hungarian, moved on from thermodynamics to nuclear chain reaction before joining Fermi and others in the awesome labour of constructing the atomic bomb.[18]

The making of the A-bomb involved huge expenditure and a wide range of other talents, ranging from the theoretical contributions of the Dane Niels Bohr on the model of the atom to the organisational abilities of the American general Leslie Groves. J. Robert Oppenheimer, dubbed 'a real genius' by Groves, combined scientific understanding with practical management of the 'Manhattan Project'. Unlike several of his colleagues, Oppenheimer was not a winner of the Nobel Prize set up by the Swedish explosives manufacturer. But he was to be among the first witnesses of a detonation-dwarfing dynamite, which brought to his mind the declaration of the Hindu God Vishnu in the *Bhagavad-Gita*: 'Now I become Death, the destroyer of worlds.' Roosevelt's elderly secretary of war, Henry L. Stimson was inspired to jot down with his own italics:

Its *size* and *character*
We don't think it *mere* new *weapon*
Revolutionary Discovery of Relation of man to universe
Great History Landmark like
    Gravitation
    Copernican Theory

But,
Bids fair *infinitely greater*, in *respect* to its *Effect*
- on the ordinary affairs of man's life.
May *destroy* or *perfect* International *Civilization*
May *Frankenstein or* means for World Peace [19]

How right Stimson was!

In the Soviet Union, where development of the bomb moved forward more slowly before 1945, a visionary comparable to Robert Oppenheimer was Vladimir Vernadsky, who wrote in 1922: 'We are approaching a great revolution in the life of humankind, with which none of those it has experienced before can be compared. The time is not far off when man will get atomic energy in his hands... Will man be able to use this power, direct it towards good, and not towards self-destruction?' Vernadsky carried on working in increasingly restrictive conditions, developing the concept of the biosphere and adopting the concept of the 'noosphere' during a spell in France. 'The noosphere is a new geological phenomenon on our planet', he wrote, continuing: 'In it for the first time man becomes a powerful geological force. He can and should restructure by his labor and thought the sphere of his life, restructure [it] radically by comparison with what went before.' He noted that since the eighteenth century man had increased greatly the quantity of biogenic gases, adding: 'Humans cutting down forests and fields...change the face of the planet, create numberless new physical-chemical processes in the history of the biosphere, until now acting more or less unconsciously. In the noosphere, the regulating of this function of humans must be one of the basic features of its new structure.'

In 1940, Vernadsky became deputy chairman of a newly-created commission on the Uranium problem. However, although the scientists had a considerable understanding of the research being carried out in the USA, it was not until January 1946 that Stalin declared it necessary to move forward the atomic project 'decisively'.[20]

Another big idea due to emerge fully after 1945, although not on the scale of the 'noosphere', was that of continental drift. Building on the work of Alfred Wegener, the geologist Arthur Holmes produced a detailed account, in the words of John Gribbin, of 'how convection currents operating inside the Earth as a result of heat generated by radio-active decay could have caused the breakup of

Pangea [the original motherland], first into two large land masses...
which in turn fragmented and drifted to form the pattern of land that
we see on the surface of the Earth today'. But Holmes himself clearly
recognised in 1944 that 'purely speculative ideas of this kind, specially
invented to match the requirements, can have no scientific value until
they acquire support from independent evidence'.[21]

Equally, scientific research cannot proceed without speculative ideas
and extraneous sources of inspiration. In a lecture that he was to give in
1960, Niels Bohr recommended an unfinished novel (1824–) entitled *En
Dansk Students Eventyr (The Adventures of a Danish Student)* by Poul Martin
Møller. He quoted the 'philosophical meditations' of one of the main
characters on the multiplicity of identity: 'I do not know at which "I"
to stop as the actual, and in the moment I stop at one, there is indeed
again an "I" which stops at it. I become confused and feel a dizziness
as if I were looking down into a bottomless abyss.' Bohr sought escape
from the abyss and infinite introspection in his work.[22]

Similarly, Leo Szilard asserted that his 'addiction to the truth' and
his predilection for 'Saving the World' came from stories his mother
told him and from a Hungarian classic, *The Tragedy of Man*, written
after the failure of the 1848 revolution by a world-weary nobleman,
Imre Madach. A long poem describes the progress through history of
Adam with Lucifer as his guide, concluding with the sun setting as only
a few Eskimos are surviving. For Szilard, at the end, 'there remains a
rather narrow margin of hope.' Later, his imagination, and perhaps
his hope, was stimulated by his reading of H. G. Wells, in particular by
two works: *The Open Conspiracy* (1928) which describes the establishment
of a world republic by enlightened industrialists and financiers; and
The World Set Free (1914), which describes a war breaking out in 1956,
destroying the major cities through the use of atomic bombs but then
using atomic energy to allow human escape from the solar system.[23]

More simply, following the death of a beloved brother, Enrico
Fermi did not look back after buying at a bookstall a two-volume
work, *Elementorum physicae mathematicae*, produced by a Jesuit physicist in
1840. In a more complex fashion, Robert Oppenheimer wrote poems
and short stories while an undergraduate at Harvard, reading widely
through T. S. Eliot's *The Waste Land* (1922) to Hindu philosophy as well
as *Principia Mathematica* (1910–13) by Bertrand Russell and Alfred North
Whitehead. He listed disparate works as his studies of metaphysics:
'the bhagavad gita, Ecclesiastes, the Stoa, the beginning of the Laws,

Hugo of St. Victor, St Thomas, John of the Cross, Spinoza'. He went through Marx, Engels and Feuerbach, but commented: 'I never accepted Communist dogma or theory; in fact, it never made sense to me.' His choice of the term 'Trinity' for the first A-bomb test site was influenced by the sonnet of John Donne beginning 'Batter my heart, three person'd God…'[24] At the time of the actual test, as already noted, Oppenheimer resorted to the declaration of the Hindu god Vishnu in the *Bhagavad-Gita*.

The development and the use of the atom bomb led to the most awesome events in human history so far.

Conclusion

In retrospect, the road from the First World War to the second might seem direct enough after the failure of the Versailles–Washington system to preserve the peace. Some analysts have seen the period from 1914 to 1945 as a European Civil War, while for others a global framework is more appropriate. Certainly, observations about stadial development from 1921 to 1945 are not easy to make even today, partly because of the continued exaggeration of the role of individuals, partly because of the world's fragmentation. The old European categories of lord and peasant, bourgeois and proletarian continued to exist, but were no longer as broadly applicable as before 1914, even within the confines of the continent. For example, the situation of workers in Germany, Italy, France, Britain and the Soviet Union differed widely. In Germany and Italy, the labour force was subject to an unprecedented degree to regimentation, while in the Soviet Union the Five-Year Plans brought comprehensive turmoil. Certainly, humankind was finding it difficult to manage the transition to the advanced industrial stage of economic development, even in the democracies in Europe and over the ocean, before the making and use of the A-bomb posed a large question mark over the future in general. Art reflected life in the disparate movement known as modernism, comprising a wide range of experiment breaking with tradition, seeking new meaning. As for those charged with the task of recording and analysing the past as it unfolded, historians between the wars found it impossible to realise the promise of a new history made at the beginning of the twentieth century: during the war, the promise was dashed completely.

Chapter 6

SUPERPOWER, 1945–1968

Superpower

Everybody should have fully realised after the A-bomb attacks on Hiroshima and Nagasaki that world history had entered a new age. However, scientists appear to have understood the new situation more completely than statesmen, and even they began to disagree among themselves about how to proceed. The scientists dilemma was expressed in different ways by J. Robert Oppenheimer and Edward Teller. At first, they appear to have agreed that further research could not be stopped, that, as Teller put it, they should not try 'to say how to tie the little toe of the ghost to the bottle from which we had just allowed it to escape'. However, while Oppenheimer continued to work for international understanding and restraint, Teller's anti-communism and Russophobia came to convince him that the USA should pursue its own research.

In November 1945, Oppenheimer gave a speech to fellow scientists at Los Alamos. 'It is not possible to be a scientist', he argued, 'unless you believe that the knowledge of the world, and the power which this gives, is a thing which is of intrinsic value to humanity, and that you are using to help in the spread of knowledge, and are willing to take the consequences'. He went on to say 'that atomic weapons are a peril which affects everyone in the world, and in that sense a completely common problem, as common a problem as it was for the Allies to defeat the Nazis'. To the argument that there were many parts of the world in which one of the deepest American beliefs, democracy, did not exist, he responded that there was 'something more profound than that; namely, the common bond with other men everywhere'. Oppenheimer turned for an analogy to one of the policies of Abraham Lincoln. Although he thought that 'there was no evil on earth more degrading than human slavery', as president he did not declare war on this issue because he realised that beyond it 'was the issue of the community of the people of this country, and the issue of the Union'. Implicitly, then, Oppenheimer was urging his fellow Americans to subordinate their deeply-held faith in democracy to the overriding task of saving the whole of humankind.

Teller took a different tack in 1949 after appearing to be in broad agreement with Oppenheimer for several years. As late as July 1948, he declared that 'World government is our only hope for survival.' He went on to argue that opposition to 'the menace of this fabulous monster, Russia…should not cause us to forget that in the long run we cannot win by working against something'. But then, after the Soviet Union's takeover of Czechoslovakia in the winter of 1948, an 'election' in May 1949 in his native Hungary confirmed the control of the Communist Party, and cut him off from his father, mother and family. Teller was back at work in Los Alamos by the time that Truman announced the explosion of 'Joe I', the first Soviet A-bomb in September 1949, while in October Mao Zedong proclaimed the triumph of the People's Republic of China, which soon set out to produce its own bomb. In January 1950, in spite of the arguments of Oppenheimer and others to the contrary, Truman opted for the development of the American H-bomb, of which Teller came to be known as the father, taking over paternity from Oppenheimer – the father of the A-bomb.[1]

The road to 'Joe I' began before 1945, as we have seen in the previous chapter. However, undoubtedly, the shock of Hiroshima and Nagasaki accelerated the process. Stalin had not previously heeded the advice of Soviet scientists, but he could not ignore the awesome demonstrations of destruction in the two Japanese cities. He now demanded that, making as much use as possible of the knowledge gained from espionage, the USSR catch up and overtake the USA, no matter what the cost. Tragically, this was to be not just a matter of roubles but also of health and safety. The dangers of radiation became apparent as the news leaked out that scientists and fellow citizens had become affected by sickness and cancer at Cheliabinsk-40 and other secret cities set apart for work on the bomb. A vast amount of radioactive waste had been discharged into river systems, exposing tens of thousands of unsuspecting local inhabitants to unseen dangers. The ecological consequences of atomic development in the USSR and elsewhere would be felt for many thousands of years.

While research on the A-bomb was conducted in private, there was no secret about the threat that it posed. Soon after the USA first successfully tested the H-bomb in 1952, for example, the leading Soviet scientist Igor Kurchatov and some colleagues published an article declaring that there could be no defence against such a weapon, and its mass production could 'create on the whole globe conditions impossible for life'. 'One cannot but acknowledge', they concluded, 'that over the human race there hangs the threat of an end to all life on earth'. However, the Soviet Union proceeded to the detonation of its own H-bomb in 1953. Then at Harwell, England in April 1956 Kurchatov suggested international collaboration in research on controlled fusion. In 1958, he supported the efforts made by another prominent scientist Andrei Sakharov to persuade Khrushchev not to renew nuclear weapons tests.[2]

After Kurchatov's death in 1960, Sakharov assumed the role of spokesman for the Soviet scientific community that culminated in 1968 in the publication of his *Reflections on Progress, Peaceful Coexistence and Intellectual Freedom*. Here, he wrote that:

> The views of the author were formed in the milieu of the scientific and scientific-technical intelligentsia, which manifests much anxiety over the principles and specific aspects of foreign and domestic policy and over the future of mankind. This anxiety is nourished, in particular, by a realization that the scientific method of directing policy, the economy, arts, education and military affairs still has not become a reality. We regard as 'scientific' a method based on deep analysis of facts, theories and views, presupposing unprejudiced, unfearing open discussion and conclusions.[3]

Sakharov's argument about the special responsibility of the scientist was similar to that put forward by Oppenheimer in 1945 – reflected in the creation of the Doomsday Clock in 1947 – and the series of international Pugwash Conferences on Science and World Affairs beginning in 1957. In 1960, Frank Drake injected further seriousness into the debate with the formulation of an equation stating that the lack of evidence for extraterrestrial civilisations suggested that civilisations based on technology tended to destroy themselves rather quickly.

From the inception of the American project leading to the first explosion in 1952, the H-bomb was known as the 'Super'. But, although it could have been, this was not the origin of the term 'superpower', which in fact made its appearance as early as 1926. Then, it was defined as the 'systematic grouping and interconnection of existing power systems',[4] apt enough for later usage but in fact referring then to the working of an electricity grid. In a political sense, W. T. R. Fox adopted the term in a book published in 1944 with the title, *The Super-Powers.* Erroneously, Fox included Britain in his subtitle along with the USA and the Soviet Union.[5] Although it was to develop its own A-bomb and H-bomb, Britain was a client of the USA during the years of the cold war, especially as its empire collapsed in the parallel years of decolonisation. It did not possess the three basic attributes of a superpower: the independent ability to destroy the world; the development of an economy sufficient for this purpose whilst at the same time maintaining socio-political stability; and the possession and dissemination of a universal ideology – either democracy or communism as first enunciated by Woodrow Wilson and V. I. Lenin on the basis of an evolutionary process beginning in the age of the Enlightenment.

The Soviet Union found it impossible to keep up with its more affluent rival, for 'superpowerdom' was an expensive business, and only those able and willing to spend vast amounts of money on armaments could attempt to maintain this status. Economic overstretch was one of the main reasons for the collapse of the Soviet Union, along with the decline of confidence in communism. In the USA, meanwhile, being a superpower was not easily compatible with the mantra of the free market. No less an authority than President Eisenhower warned his fellow citizens in his famous farewell speech of January 1961 to 'guard against the acquisition of unwarranted influence, whether sought or unsought, by the military–industrial complex. The potential for the disastrous rise of misplaced power exists and will persist.'[6]

The military–industrial complex was a mixed blessing for science, providing ready support for research ranging from outer space to ocean floors when it promoted strategic advantage but to the comparative neglect of more peaceful enterprise. Nevertheless, 'disillusioned with physics as a result of seeing its application to war', Francis Crick joined with James Watson and Maurice Wilkins to engage in research that gained them a Nobel prize in 1962 for their contribution to the revelation of the double-helix structure of deoxyribonucleic acid (DNA). This was to lead to an expanding amount of research in the 1960s and after, clarifying the picture of 'how science has altered humankind's perception of our own place in nature'.[7]

The Cold War and Decolonisation

As a consequence of the Second World War, there could be no more talk of a balance of power arranged exclusively by European diplomats. For now, by a wide margin, the USA was the global power, with the Soviet Union in second place largely because of its occupation of a vast amount of strategically-situated land. The situation was well expressed in 1950 by the American journalist Howard K. Smith:

> The nation that has expanded most since the outbreak of World War II has not been Russia, but America. The most distant of Russia's new areas of dominance are 600 miles from her borders. The farthest of America's are 7,000 miles. Since 1942, America has displaced Britain as ruler of the seas, including that most British of all waters, the eastern Mediterranean. America is said to have a lien on some 400 world-wide naval and air bases. This means that any empire linked to its motherland by water exists on American sufferance, as it did in the past on British sufferance. Russian influence over other governments is blatantly visible. American influence is like an iceberg: only the smaller part can readily be seen by the naked eye.[8]

Two interconnected processes, the cold war and decolonisation, were to give new emphasis to the downfall of Europe.

While Europe welcomed American dollars, it attempted to resist the USA's cultural influence. 'It's true they have the money bags, But we have all the brains' said a note circulating within the British delegation to the postwar loan talks,[9] anticipating the more dignified but no less arrogant observation of Harold Macmillan that the UK constituted Greece to the USA's Rome. France made a strong comeback with the development of the philosophy of existentialism by Jean-Paul Sartre and others. But many of the world's leading artists and scientists were attracted to the USA, where high culture flourished, too, with the open and clandestine support of the government. Moreover, the vigour and persistence of transatlantic cinema and popular song could not be ignored, any more than the military and economic might. With the advent of television, American mass culture became more pervasive throughout the world.

Arguably, the cold war had been on the way for some time, even for about a century-and-a-half, especially to the extent that it involved a confrontation between America and Russia. From at least the late eighteenth century, astute observers could discern that these two future superpowers on Europe's flanks were heading towards a shared dominance of the world amid probable conflict. Such an observation is reinforced in the context of the realisation that these two new empires were rising up on the shoulders of the old. Britain, France and other European states were losing not only their continental but also their overseas influence to these rivals, who struggled with each other to fill up as much as possible of the resulting power vacuum. To put it simply, the cold war was intimately linked with decolonisation, the other principal characteristic of the years following 1945.

At the very most, Soviet aggressive postures were at first confined to Eastern Europe and other lands contiguous to the USSR, while President Truman had at his disposal not only the atomic bomb but also the express desire 'to preserve the peace of the world'.[10] Undoubtedly, too, the USA was in a dominant financial position, as its former allies had discovered at a conference at Bretton Woods, New Hampshire in July 1944. An International Monetary Fund (IMF) and an International Bank for Reconstruction and Development (IBRD, World Bank) were set up in such a manner that the other trading currencies were effectively tied to the dollar. Lord Keynes complained after attending a further conference of the two new agencies at Savannah, Georgia in March 1946: 'I went expecting to meet the world and all I met was a tyrant.'[11] Similarly, the United Nations Relief and Recovery Administration (UNRRA) and other such agencies were dependent largely on American finance, and so the American influence in their administration was greatest.

In spite of references to the 'iron curtain' by Churchill and others even before his famous speech of March 1946, the cold war did not break out fully until 1947, when European imperial power in general was in steep decline and Britain in particular conceded that it no longer had the strength to help maintain order in the Mediterranean.[12] In what became known as the Truman Doctrine, the president declared that thenceforth it must be American policy 'to support free peoples who are resisting attempted subjugation by armed minorities or outside pressures... If we falter, we may endanger the peace of the world and we shall surely endanger the welfare of our own Nation.'[13] Less than three months after the enunciation of the Truman Doctrine, the Marshall Plan comprised a scheme of long-term recovery for European civilisation through integration and planning backed by American aid.

Like the cold war, decolonisation had deep historical roots. Its first moment could be said to have been the American Declaration of Independence of 1776. The nature of its creation gave the USA a sense of moral superiority over not only Britain but also all European imperial powers. To be sure, as we have seen, the USA participated in the nineteenth-century competition for empire, exterminating Native Americans and occupying foreign territory, though with more soul-searching than its rivals normally felt necessary. Thus, American statesmen felt justified in preaching decolonisation after 1945 as their own influence spread around the world. They were joined by their Soviet counterparts, heirs to the tsarist empire and enthusiasts for its extension, but proclaimers of Marxist-Leninist doctrines of self-determination. At Yalta, as if both he and the Soviet leader were innocent of imperialist policies, Roosevelt advised Stalin not to mention the sensitive subject of Indian independence to Churchill.

Before that aspiration became event in 1947, Nehru even-handedly observed: 'All the evils of a purely political democracy are evident in the USA; the evils of the lack of political democracy are present in the USSR.'[14] Afterwards, he attempted to make India part of a third force between capitalism and communism. The Chinese Revolution of 1949 complicated both decolonisation and the cold war further, at first during the Korean War (1950–3). The twin processes continued through to 1968, when there was serious reappraisal. On the way, the most important milestones were the Cuban Crisis of 1962, which brought the superpowers to the brink of war, and the American intervention in Vietnam from 1964, influenced by the rising power of China which had acquired the H-Bomb by 1967.

Another New History?

The Second World War could not fail to make a huge impact on historians, especially those on the losing side. For example, Friedrich Meinecke, who had written of nationalism as the highest form of universalism before the First World War and sought a new relativist rationale in interwar Germany, now asserted in *Die Deutsche Katastrophe* of 1946 that history was a matter of blind chance.[15] However, in retrospect, it appears strange that the A-bomb exerted so little immediate influence on the writing of history. There were perhaps two main reasons for this: one was the innate conservatism of historians, determined to pursue their work in a traditional manner; the other was the impact of the cold war, which distracted historians from what could, even should, have been a major consideration. For the same reasons, historians gave little consideration to ecological problems, even though at least one of them showed a clear understanding of their imminence. In 1949, Arthur M. Schlesinger wrote:

> The human race may shortly be confronted by an entirely new range of problems – problems of naked subsistence whose solution will require the combined efforts of all people if the race is to survive. We have raped the earth too long, and we are paying the price today in the decline of fertility. Industrial society has disturbed the balance of nature, and no one can estimate the consequences... In the light of this epic struggle to restore man to his foundations in nature, the political conflicts which obsess us today seem puny and flickering.

Yet Schlesinger had no doubt of the Wilsonian manner in which these conflicts should be resolved: 'Unless we are soon able to make the world safe for democracy, we may commit ourselves too late to the great and final struggle to make the world safe for humanity.'[16]

Let us investigate postwar historiography more closely, beginning with the Englishman R. G. Collingwood's contribution. In *An Autobiography* published in 1939, Collingwood had declared that 'The chief business of twentieth-century philosophy is to reckon with twentieth-century history.' As far as the study of history was concerned, he insisted that 'In the last thirty or forty years historical thought had been achieving an acceleration in the velocity of its progress and an enlargement in its outlook comparable to those which natural science had achieved about the beginning of the seventeenth century.' He continued by claiming that 'We might very well be standing on the threshold of an age in which history would be as important for the world as natural science had been between 1600 and 1900.' He claimed that 'The historian's business is to reveal the less obvious features hidden from a careless eye in the present situation. What history can bring to moral and political life is a trained eye for the situation in which one has to act.' Collingwood's own trained eye led him on to the assertion that 'historical knowledge is the re-enactment in the historian's mind of the thought whose history he is studying'. Furthermore, 'what is miscalled an 'event' is really an action, and expresses some thought (intention, purpose) of its agent; the historian's business is therefore to identify this thought.' Collingwood confessed to difficulties with his own identity, but the Spanish Civil War convinced him that Fascism meant 'the end of clear thinking and the triumph of irrationalism'. On Marxism, he was more sympathetic, although not uncritical. He concluded that throughout his whole life he had been 'engaged unawares in a political struggle, fighting against these things in the dark. Henceforth I shall fight in the daylight'.[17] After Collingwood died in 1943, *The Idea of History*, elaborating ideas outlined in *An Autobiography* was assembled and published six years later. Collingwood found many admirers, but few disciples, although his arguments were possibly to find some reassertion years later in the postmodernist movement.[18]

A multivolumed work with that very title, *A Study of History*, begun by Arnold Toynbee in 1934, was completed by him in 1954. A bold, erudite and imaginative analysis of the rise and fall of civilisations governed by a number of historical laws, including challenge-and-response, Toynbee's work achieved considerable popularity in the years following the Second World War, rather like Spengler's *The Decline of the West* after the first. The renewed suggestion that, in its turn, Western civilisation might follow its predecessors into decline gave much pause for thought. Among the other reasons for *A Study*'s success, apart from its sheer scale, was its implication, especially in the later volumes, that 'universal states' might constitute 'means towards something beyond them'. Toynbee wrote, for example: 'we may and must pray that a reprieve which God has granted to our society once will not be refused if we ask for it again in a humble spirit and a contrite heart'.[19] His reputation grew to such an extent by 1947 that *Time* magazine celebrated *A Study of History* as a transformation of history from Ptolemaic to Copernican as it 'shattered the frozen patterns of historical determinism and materialism by again asserting God as an active force in history'.[20] Denounced during the existence of the Soviet Union, Toynbee became popular in Russia, too, after its fall, with some of his readers no doubt finding in his work an explanation of what had happened to them.

Across the Channel, there was a continuation of the *Annales* school, founded by Marc Bloch and Lucien Febvre in 1920 in the wake of the 'synthesis' movement begun in 1900 by Henri Berr. During the Second World War, Marc Bloch was first imprisoned and then executed for his membership of the resistance movement. He left behind him an unfinished work, translated into English as *The Historian's Craft*, recommending that sciences advance 'as they deliberately abandon the old anthropocentrism of good and evil'. Bloch wrote:

> Today, we should laugh at a chemist who separated the bad gases, like chlorine, from the good ones like oxygen. But, had chemistry adopted this classification in its infancy, it would have run the grave risk of getting stuck there, to the great detriment of the knowledge of matter.

Of course, he observed, the science of man differed from the science of the physical world, adding to his view that 'the only true history, which can advance only through mutual aid, is universal history' – a passionate plea:

> When all is said and done, a single word, 'understanding', is the beacon light of our studies. Let us not say that the true historian is a stranger to emotion: he has that, at all events. 'Understanding', in all honesty, is a word pregnant with difficulties, but also with hope. Moreover, it is a friendly word. Even in action, we are far too prone to judge. It is easy to denounce. We are never sufficiently understanding. Whoever differs from us – a foreigner or a political adversary – is almost inevitably considered evil. A little more understanding of people would be necessary merely for guidance, in the conflicts which are unavoidable; all the more to prevent them while there is yet still time.[21]

After 1945, the *Annales* movement was continued most notably by Fernand Braudel. Like Henri Pirenne in the First World War, Braudel was a prisoner during the second. Like Pirenne, too, he wrote a book from memory while in captivity, in his case *The Mediterranean and the Mediterranean World in the Age of Philip II*. Braudel explained his distinctive approach in the preface of an early edition of *The Mediterranean* in 1946, declaring:

> It will perhaps prove that history can do no more than study walled gardens. If it were otherwise, it would surely be failing in one of its most immediate tasks which must be to relate to the painful problems of our times and to maintain contact with the

youthful but imperialistic human sciences. Can there be any study of humanity, in 1946, without historians who are ambitious, conscious of their duties and of their immense powers? 'It is the fear of great history which has killed great history', wrote Edmond Faral, in 1942. May it live again![22]

In a preface to an updated edition of *The Mediterranean* in 1965, Braudel concluded with the paradox that

> the true man of action is he who can measure most nearly the constraints upon him, who chooses to remain with them and even to take advantage of the weight of the inevitable, exerting his own pressure in the same direction. All efforts against the prevailing tide of history – which is not always obvious – are doomed to failure.

Whenever he thought of the individual, he was 'always inclined to see him imprisoned within a destiny in which he himself has little hand, fixed in a landscape in which the infinite perspectives of the long term stretch into the distance both behind him and before'.[23]

  Braudel believed that he could describe the predicament of the man of action, and overcome constraints on the historian, through a method that he called total history, covering all aspects of human behaviour through three approaches. 'Events, Politics and People' was 'the most exciting of all, the richest in human interest, and almost the most dangerous'. Braudel insisted:

> We must learn to distrust this history with its still burning passions, as it was felt, described, and lived by contemporaries whose lives were as short and as short-sighted as ours… Resounding events are often only momentary outbursts, surface manifestations of… larger movements and explicable only in terms of them.[24]

Critics would be justified in saying that the 'momentary outbursts' of the A-bomb over Hiroshima and Nagasaki were much more significant than any events occurring in the sixteenth century. Nevertheless, there is a strong case for considering Braudel's 'larger movements'. One of these was 'Collective Destinies and General Trends', concerning economic systems, states, societies, civilisations and forms of war. The other was 'The Role of the Environment', which Braudel described as 'almost

timeless history…in which all change is slow, a history of constant
repetition, ever-recurring cycles', involving human contact with the
inanimate   land, sea and climate, communications and cities.[25] By the
end of the twentieth century, the environment would be widely seen as
playing a different role, unfortunately no longer timeless. Nevertheless,
the Braudelian approach – summarised as event, conjuncture and
structure – could be applied to the study of the cold war in a profitable
if limited manner.[26]

The Cold War and History

To what extent did the threat of an atomic war that was posed by the
cold war influence the approach of historians to their subject? An
appropriate example to take here is the British historian A. J. P. Taylor.
A member of the Campaign for Nuclear Disarmament, Taylor was
most concerned with the period before the Second World War. After
considering *The Course of German History* (1945), the coherent view
of a victor from the outside in contrast to the defeated Meinecke's
fragmented reaction from inside, Taylor turned to *The Struggle for
Mastery in Europe* (1954), building on his prewar work. Most controversial
was *The Origins of the Second World War*, first published in 1961, in
which he argued that Hitler's foreign policy emerged from previous
German and European history rather than from the man himself.
In particular, Taylor asserted that 'in one form or another Germany,
remaining united at the end of the First World War, was bound to
seek to undo the Treaty of Versailles; and that the impetus of success
in undoing this Treaty would carry Germany forward, unless it was
checked in some way, into being again a great and dominant power in
Europe.' Nevertheless, Taylor wrote, 'The war of 1939, far from being
premeditated, was a mistake, the result on both sides of diplomatic
blunders.' If the Second World War was a mistake or accident, what
hope could there be for avoiding a third? Consequently, Taylor said,
'Liking the book becomes a matter of politics. If you're a Left Winger
and against the bomb and the arming of Germany, you may be in
sympathy with the thesis; if you're a conservative, a militarist, and for
Germany in NATO, you may not be.'[27]

     In 1952, the first number of a new journal was published with
the title *Past and Present*. It grew out of the discussions of the British
Communist Party Historians' Group, but, according to some of its

founders, its aim was to draw the line 'between what we saw as a minority of committed historical (and political) conservatives, not to mention the anti-Communist crusaders, and a potentially large body of those who had a common approach to history, whether they were Marxists or not'. Nevertheless, 'the initial subtitle *A Journal of Scientific History*, which expressed the belief that historical phenomena have an objective existence and may be studied by the methods of reason and science, was to arouse ideological suspicion some years later among those who thought it a synonym for Marxism'. It was dropped in 1958 at the insistence of new members of the editorial board 'without significant resistance by any of the founders, and without any discernible effect on the content of the journal'.[28] However, one of the new members, Lawrence Stone, claimed later that 'neo-Marxists' seemed to have abandoned any pretension to 'scientific history'.[29]

Certainly, in 1950, Conyers Read had set an appropriate tone for the cold war in a presidential address to the American Historical Association entitled 'The Social Responsibilities of the Historian'. According to Read:

> Discipline is the essential prerequisite of every effective army whether it march under the Stars and Stripes or under the Hammer and Sickle. We have to fight an enemy whose value system is deliberately simplified in order to achieve quick decisions. And atomic bombs make quick decisions imperative. The liberal neutral attitude, the approach to social evolution in terms of dispassionate behaviourism will no longer suffice. Dusty answers will not satisfy our demands for positive assurances. Total war, whether it be hot or cold, enlists everyone and calls upon everyone to assume his part. The historian is no freer from this obligation than the physicist.

'This sounds like the advocacy of one form of social control against another', Read confessed, continuing: 'In short, it is. But I see no alternative in a divided world.'[30]

In fact, as we have seen above, at least some physicists did see an alternative. Already in 1945 already J. Robert Oppenheimer had responded to the observation that there were parts of the world where American beliefs, democracy, did not exist, with the insistence that there was 'something more profound than that; namely, the common bond with other men everywhere'. In 1968, Andrei Sakharov was to voice a long-held belief: 'We consider "scientific" that method which is based on a profound study of facts, theories and views, presupposing unprejudiced and open discussion, which is dispassionate in its conclusions.'[31]

But there was no shortage of American historians in tacit agreement with their colleague Conyers Read as the cold war unfolded, ready to condemn Stalin's expansionist ambitions at every opportunity. This was in spite of the actual situation, with American influence spreading throughout the world, while its Soviet counterpart was confined largely to Eastern Europe. One major reason for the influence of the USA appearing less perceptible was that most American citizens looked upon it as benign and not needing special attention. Even right-wing dictators in Latin America and elsewhere could be tolerated in the fortress of democracy, provided that they were vigorous opponents of communism. As Roosevelt famously said of the Dominican Republic's Rafael Trujillo: he was 'an s.o.b.' but 'our s.o.b.'[32]

Consequently, during the first years of the cold war, US historiography attributed the conflict to Soviet, especially Stalinist, aggression. Then, during the 1950s, some critics argued that Franklin D. Roosevelt and other wartime Western statesmen had trusted Stalin and his henchmen when their suspicions should have been aroused by early Soviet behaviour. The accusation of appeasement, first levelled against the men of Munich before the war, was revived with new force: there could not now be peace with honour, and the conciliatory, hesitant policies at the end of the war and afterwards had led to the advance of the Red Tide in Europe and Asia. In this spirit, Foster Rhea Dulles, cousin of the secretary of state and leading diplomatic historian, wrote that, as the USA began to assume imperial responsibilities around 1900, the people developed 'doubts and misgivings as to whether the nation had set out on the right course'. Only the 'dreadful experience' of the two world wars, Dulles continued, drove home lessons that should have been learned before, and the debate on empire around 1900 had assumed 'an unexpected relevancy for a day in which the United States has assumed the obligations and made the commitments it so long refused'.[33]

Other critics, the so-called 'realists', asserted that American governments had been motivated too much by moralistic and idealistic considerations and not enough by the world as it actually was and national interests as they should have been. In particular, more attention should be given to the opportunist, traditional and limited elements in

Soviet policy. Then, from about the mid-1960s, as we shall see in the next chapter, a revisionist school often labelled as the 'New Left' arose.[34]

On the other side, the orthodox Soviet view was put forward in 1947 by D. Voblikov:

> The Truman Doctrine concerning the world domination of the USA supplemented and made concrete in the so-called Marshall Plan, places that country in the forefront of world imperialism and reaction. American monopolistic capital, enriched by the excess profits of the war years and emboldened to the extreme, has led an offensive against the popular masses within the country and against the progressive forces of the whole world... The new addition to the Monroe Doctrine [in Latin America] combines hypocrisy and brutal coercion, the policy of the dollar, and the policeman's club, spreading this policy throughout the world.[35]

After the death of Stalin, a 'thaw' set in, but the room for manoeuvre of Soviet historians remained severely limited, and individual scholars were disciplined for what appeared from outside to be no more than minor deviation. For example, just after Khrushchev's 'secret speech' of February 1956 criticising Stalin's excesses, the historian E. N. Burdzhalov was demoted for an article pointing out that in the spring of 1917 Stalin was an associate of two 'traitors' later executed during his purges.

Decolonisation and History

Decolonisation was a significant part of the European imperial experience as a whole. However, sometimes its importance has been exaggerated, with more emphasis given to the formal transfer of power than to the incorporation of the newly independent states in wider networks of influence, communist or capitalist. For example, as John Kent points out, 'attempts to incorporate the role of Western capitalism in Central Africa and in the ongoing interactions of the Cold War and decolonisation have generally been neglected'. Some American administrations gave high priority to Central Africa. To quote Kent again: 'Not the Soviet Union nor China nor the countries of Western Europe ever generated anything like the same amount of paper as the Congo which under Kennedy was only exceeded by Vietnam.' Under Johnson, even more emphasis was given to Vietnam.[36]

President Johnson also enunciated the 'Johnson Doctrine' according to which the president could use force whenever he believed that communism was threatening the West. Johnson was not alone. It was a consistent American policy to intervene in Latin America to protect business as well as security, whether directly through sending in the armed forces or indirectly, by training local police and military. As Odd Arne Westad has observed: 'While the US domination of Latin America was…developing out of processes that began well before 1945, the Cold War gave shape and direction to attempts at the systematic subordination of the states on the southern half of the continent to the will of the United States.'[37]

The earlier historiography of decolonisation may appropriately be introduced by looking at the contribution of the Dutch historian Jan Romein. Calling himself a Marxist, but following no party line, Romein increased his reputation in 1945 with an article on 'Theoretical History', the outline of a course that he proposed for the University of Amsterdam. Not obviously Marxist, and indeed recommending Toynbee's *A Study of History* as an example of what could be achieved, the article echoed Collingwood's argument that the structure of even the simplest historical event originates in the mind of the historian.[38] However, Romein's professed political allegiance was enough for a visa for travel to the USA to be refused (as well as for his reputation to be less widespread than that of Pieter Geyl and other colleagues). Instead, he went to newly independent Indonesia, where he collected material for another article published in 1957–8 on 'The Common Human Pattern', or CHP.

For Romein, the CHP had six distinguishing characteristics: *nature* – feeling part of it, knowing how to make use of it when necessary but not seeking to dominate it; *life* – accepting that it is essentially worthless, a transition to another existence in the cosmic whole; *thought* – in images not concepts, concretely not abstractly, with much less interest in conscious organisation, in church or state; *time* – 'but a succession of todays', with no saving of time, or capital, or any conception of progress; *authority* – of the gods, the prince, the father, the teacher and the book, either absolute or non-existent; *work* – a necessary evil, the very word signifying worry and pain, and no work ethic or worship as in the West. It was Western divergence from the CHP that had allowed extraordinary progress. This process had been followed from Greece and Rome through the reception of Christianity, the Renaissance and the Enlightenment, developing reason, organisation and individualism.

Fifty years on from its publication, the article on 'The Common Human Pattern' appears patronising in the extreme towards the non-Western peoples of the world, as well as wildly inaccurate in view of the later rise of Japan, China and India. It could be introduced into the continuing discussion of the extent to which the process of modernisation may be deemed to be Westernisation.[39]

Let us turn from Jan Romein, who called himself a Marxist, to E. H. Carr, who was called a Marxist by others. In 1961, in chapter 6 of *What Is History?*, entitled 'The Widening Horizon', Carr gave some emphasis to the changed shape of the world, noting that 'Western Europe, together with the outlying parts of the English-speaking world, has become an appanage of the North American continent, or, if you like, an agglomeration in which the United States serves both as powerhouse and as control-tower.' Moreover, he added:

It is by no means clear that the world centre of gravity now resides, or will continue for long to reside, in the English-speaking world with its western European annex. It appears to be the great land-mass of eastern Europe and Asia, with its extensions into Africa, which today calls the tune in world affairs. The 'unchanging east' is nowadays a singularly worn-out cliché.

Nearly half a century on, approaching twenty years after the collapse of the Soviet Union, the world centre of gravity still appears to reside in the USA and its annex, but appearances could be deceptive, for the East is changing even faster than in 1961.[40]

Genuine Marxists, as opposed to Romein and Carr, would be able to present a more coherent, if not necessarily more accurate, view of the world undergoing the twin experiences of the cold war and decolonisation. But which Marxists were genuine?

Back in the autumn of 1947, E. V. Tarle noted that there would soon be two significant anniversaries: 800 years since the founding of Moscow as capital of a great state, and 30 years since the transformation of that state into a socialist power. How many exciting comparisons, how many ideas were evoked by the thought of these happily coincidental celebrations, he continued, among them the occasions during the country's 1,100 year history when Russian military might had helped to save Europe, for example following the Napoleonic invasion of 1812. Tarle conceded that at other times that same military might had been used in a manner more threatening to Europe. However, he insisted, the Great October Socialist Revolution had produced a much greater power, devoted exclusively to progress. He concluded: 'The struggle for the preservation of peace between peoples and for the social progress of humankind is now associated throughout the world with the image of Moscow, old and new, and of a mighty world power of which the Kremlin is the heart and brain.'[41] In the West, of course, the image of the Kremlin was very different.

So was the appraisal of Soviet Marxism in a global context. In 1962, the American sociologist C. Wright Mills wrote that two overwhelming facts had to be faced: first, no advanced capitalist society had seen a successful proletarian revolution; second, Bolshevik-type revolutions avowedly Marxist had succeeded only in backward peasant societies. Moreover, Marx himself could write little about the course to be taken by proletarian revolution since capitalism had not developed sufficiently to produce it by the time of his death in 1883. Therefore, Lenin and his successors had to put forward their own arguments. At a different stage of development, China was also interpreting Marxist ideology in its own way.[42] Censuring Western Marxism for its '*lack of internationalism*', Perry Anderson also criticises its esotericism and remoteness from '*actual masses*'.[43] More of this in the next chapter.

Conclusion

Neither the ideology of American capitalism nor Soviet socialism was worried about saving the planet, dependent as they both were on exploitation of human and natural resources and continual growth. Although it is difficult to say exactly when such concern began, the publication in 1952 of *The Sea Around Us* by the American biologist Rachel Carson was undoubtedly an important milestone. Her following work, *Silent Spring* in 1962, was even more significant, containing the warning:

> We are subjecting whole populations to exposure to chemicals which animal experiments have proved to be extremely poisonous and, in many cases, cumulative in their effects. These exposures now begin at or before birth and, unless we change our methods, will continue through the lifetime of those now living.

The particular target of Carson's attack was the deleterious impact of DDT and other synthetic pesticides used to increase agricultural productivity, not only on wild life but also through the food chain on human beings.

Of course, Rachel Carson was not alone. Among other 'green' writers, the British economist Barbara Ward was one of several to use the phrase *Spaceship Earth*, the title of her book published in 1966. A specialist on poverty in the wider world, Ward found a close correlation between the distribution of the world's wealth and the conservation of its natural resources, asserting that 'the careful husbandry of the Earth is sine qua non for the survival of the human species, and for the creation of decent ways of life for all the people of the world'. More than Carson, however, Ward was aware of the great genetic discovery made in the 1950s, writing: 'We cannot cheat on DNA. We cannot get round photosynthesis. We cannot say I am not going to give a damn about phytoplankton. All these tiny mechanisms provide the preconditions of our planetary life.'[11] The message began to spread.

The year 1945 was the most significant date in history up to that point. This was realised by the scientists who had made the A-bomb, in particular by J. Robert Oppenheimer. Like many other world citizens, historians must have appreciated the significance of the moment, too, but the arrival of the cold war and, and albeit to a lesser extent, decolonisation, appears to have diverted the minds of most of them. Nevertheless, there were some advances in historical science, for example those made by Fernand Braudel in developing some of the ideas of the *Annales* school.

The independence of India in 1947 and the Chinese Revolution of 1949, along with the revival of Japan, made it clear that the world would no longer be dominated by Western empires, whose decline was reinforced by the inclusion of their European metropolitan centres in the spheres of influence of the USA and the USSR, two former empires now becoming superpowers.

Gandhi and Mao made it clear that the question of the role of the individual could no longer be mostly focused on the West. Yet this question was addressed in the most awesome fashion at the time of the Cuban Crisis of 1962 by John F. Kennedy and Nikita S. Khrushchev, when the whole world was close to the threat of an outbreak of nuclear war. Certainly, both of them showed courage at a time of mortal crisis.

But the harrowing experience that they shared did not bring a lasting halt to the arms race. The American 'military–industrial complex' about which Eisenhower had given a solemn warning in 1961 before the Cuban Crisis showed little sign of losing its influence afterwards. The implications of this fact for the ever-increasing peoples of the whole world were awesome.

Chapter 7

PLANET EARTH, 1968–1991

Globalisation

The 1968 revolution does not appear as profound now as it did then, perhaps, but it certainly encouraged the global approach to the problems facing humankind. This approach was stimulated by a previous event occurring in 1967, the detonation of a Chinese H-Bomb, which signalled the end of the Western domination of the world that began in the sixteenth century. Was China on the way to becoming a third superpower? Then, the global view received a boost in 1969 from the moon landing, which reinforced the impact of photographs taken from space showing earth and its thin coat of atmosphere in all their fragility.

Before human history began, earth's continents had drifted apart. But so-called primitive peoples were great travellers, and moved freely around and between Eurasia, the Americas, Africa and Europe before the arrival of the early civilisations. In a sense, therefore, the reverse process to continental drift, bringing the continents together again, began early. The classical and medieval periods saw significant connections, too. The Greeks and the Romans penetrated central Asia, for example, while Vikings crossed the Atlantic Ocean, Arabs reached China by sea, and the Chinese sailed to Africa. From the point of view of European discovery and colonisation in particular, the sixteenth and seventeenth centuries marked an acceleration in awareness of the world as one. This realisation developed further with the expansion of empire from the eighteenth century onwards, with the USA and Japan joining in at the end of the nineteenth century.[1]

The two world wars of the twentieth century both began in Europe but then exerted a powerful globalising influence, the first leading to the confrontation of Leninism and Wilsonism, the second promoting the emergence of the superpowers. Then, the twin process of the cold war and decolonisation was all-pervasive. Nuclear weapons proliferated, while a third industrial revolution affected all the earth's regions, superimposing new technologies on the old and necessitating further adaptations to concepts of society as well as of economy. In particular, the events of the year 1968 and the ensuing debate promoted the idea that local events interacted with others occurring thousands of miles away. An extremely important feature of this new stage in the process was the spread of news by television. For example, the fact that the Vietnam War was the first to be widely shown as well as reported had much to do with its growing unpopularity throughout the USA, Europe and the rest of the world.

From 1968 to 1991, the superpowers struggled to coexist with each other and to manage threats to their dominance. The USA appeared susceptible to imperial overstretch, including in its own backyard, Latin America. Although it continued to be the world's major currency, the dollar ceased to be almighty. Moreover, the insatiable American thirst for oil contributed to serious problems in the Middle East, the world's major supplier. Meanwhile, the USSR took overstretch to breaking point, bogged down by its own Vietnam in Afghanistan and facing insubordination at the centre of its sphere of influence in Eastern Europe, whilst at the same time trying to catch up with its rival throughout the world. But the rest of the world refused to be passive in the face of the ambitions of the superpowers. In Asia in particular, while Japan held on to its economic lead, southeastern 'tiger' economies emerged and China continued its inexorable rise. And if Western Europe no longer played the leading role, it still asserted its presence on the international stage.

The spirit of the 1980s was exuded by such individuals as presidents Gorbachev and Reagan, and the various policies of 'freedom' associated with them. Mikhail Gorbachev preached his gospel of *perestroika*, but found it difficult to follow up words with action, while events overtook him in Eastern Europe in 1989. Ronald Reagan moved from condemnation of the Soviet 'evil empire' to accommodation with Gorbachev, while assuring his fellow-countrymen that there was nothing to worry about but worry itself. In China, soon after the death of Mao in 1976, his successors opened the doors to economic freedom, but kept them firmly closed politically.

1968 and After

During the 1968 revolution, there was little loss of life, particularly in Europe, although there were certainly riots in Paris and other cities. Even the Soviet tanks sent to crush the Prague Spring were more restrained than their predecessors in Budapest in 1956. Indeed, there was a certain amount of dialogue between the Czechs and the invaders, one soldier leaning down from his turret to explain: 'Look, you are a tiny little country with tiny little problems. But we are a very, very big country with very big problems. So you can never understand why we have to be here.'[2] The highest mortality was in Mexico, where about three hundred and fifty people were killed as government troops were ordered to restore order before the opening of the Olympic Games. The Games themselves are better remembered for the black-gloved, clenched-fist protest of medal-winning Black American athletes on the victory podium. Back in the USA, Martin Luther King was assassinated in April and Robert Kennedy in June. There was much violence and destruction on many campuses, and lots of exhortation, albeit few deaths. With the use of defoliants and other pollutants in Vietnam, the green movement began to emerge. The May 1970 number of the radical journal *Ramparts* was an 'Ecology Special', catching the spirit of the time with an incendiary cover exclaiming: 'The students who burned the Bank of America in Santa Barbara may have done more towards saving the environment than all the Teach-ins put together.'

However, the overall significance of 1968 lay less in the violence of its events than in the discussion that they promoted. In a retrospective essay entitled '1968, Revolution in the World-System', published in another highly significant year, 1989, the historical sociologist Immanuel Wallerstein declared that the year 1968 brought about a revolution – a single revolution, a great, formative, watershed event – in and of the world system. Protest was primarily directed at American hegemony and Soviet acquiescence, but secondarily and more passionately against 'old left' systemic movements, in particular Stalinism, and was in favour of new ideologies, especially variants of Maoism. 1968 also brought counterculture involving lifestyles and minorities, as well as promoting debate among anti-systemic movements on the fundamental strategy of social transformation. In 1989, Wallerstein added to his analysis questions about anti-systemic movements and the possibility of significant political change without the transfer of state power, including cooperation between the

West, the Soviet bloc and the Third World. He also asked about an update of the French Revolution's 'liberty, equality, fraternity' and how plenty, or even enough, could be achieved without productivism. (Incidentally, might this also require an update of the American Revolution's 'life, liberty and the pursuit of happiness'?) In 1991, just before the collapse of the Soviet Union, Wallerstein insisted that 'The regime changes of 1989 were…the outcome of the latent, continuing revolt of 1968.'[3] Nearly twenty more years on in 2010, 1968 no longer perhaps appears to be quite such a great, formative, watershed event, but at least it lit up the essential unity of the world system.

The Club of Rome, the Brandt Commission and Gaia

In April 1968, a group composed of scientists, educators, economists, industrialists, and national and international civil servants – 30 in all and from 10 countries – met in Rome as an 'invisible college'. It had three basic aims: to promote understanding of the components forming the global system – economic, social, political and natural; to acquaint policy-makers and the public everywhere with this understanding; and thus to promote new initiatives and action. In 1970 the Club of Rome, as the group called itself, commissioned a research team at the Massachusetts Institute of Technology to prepare for publication *The Limits to Growth* (1972), a report which put new life into some of the arguments that Malthus had first advanced in the eighteenth century but had often been neglected since. By this point the club had grown to an informal association of about 70 individuals – none holding public office – of 25 nationalities.

The Limits to Growth used figures, tables and computer models to produce three conclusions: 1) that limits to growth would be reached at some point in the next 100 years with the probable result of 'a rather sudden and uncontrollable decline in both population and industrial capacity' if the current trends in population, industrialisation, pollution, food production and resource depletion were to persist; 2) that an alternative could be the establishment of sustainable ecological and economic stability and equilibrium if basic human needs and potential were designed for each person; 3) and that the sooner an attempt at the alternative was begun, the more likely its chances of success.

After presenting the findings of the MIT report at two international meetings, one in Moscow and the other in Rio de Janeiro, the Executive Committee of the Club of Rome made its own comments on what it called the report's 'pessimistic' conclusions, affirming that 'any deliberate attempt to reach a rational and enduring state of equilibrium by planned measures, rather than by chance or catastrophe, must ultimately be founded on a basic change of values and goals at individual, national, and world levels'. This change, the Executive Committee considered, was 'perhaps already in the air, however faintly'. Only through such change could the human species survive 'without falling into a state of worthless existence'.[4]

Two years after *The Limits to Growth*, another Club of Rome publication ensued in 1974 with the title *Mankind at the Turning Point*. Why so soon, and what was new? Four major conclusions were emphasised: 1) that the current crises were not temporary; 2) that they could only be resolved globally; 3) that they could not be solved by one traditional approach, for example economic; 4) and that they could be solved only by mutually beneficial cooperation rather than confrontation. Society would have to realise that short-term considerations could not fail to be counterproductive and that long-term crises were of overriding importance. Therefore, it needed to develop an appreciation of the futility of narrow nationalism and the consequent necessity of a practical international framework for cooperation. The authors observed:

> Governments and international organizations are currently too preoccupied with military alliances and bloc politics. But this problem is becoming of secondary importance, because a nuclear war could clearly result in a suicidal holocaust and can no longer be counted among rational alternatives. Therefore, barring suicide, mankind will face the most awesome test in its history: the necessity of a change in the man-nature relationship and the emergence of a new perception of mankind as a living global system.

Thus, a new global ethic was implied involving a world consciousness, the appropriate use of material resources, a harmonious attitude to nature and a sense of identification with future generations. The authors considered human prospects over a 50-year period, beyond which were the 'outer limits' that 'man cannot transgress without destroying himself and the biosphere'.[5]

The Club of Rome certainly mentioned the North-South global divide, but did not give it as much emphasis as the Brandt Commission in two reports: *North-South: A Programme for Survival*, 1979; and *Common Crisis North-South: Co-operation for World Recovery*, 1983. In his introduction to the second of these works, Willy Brandt himself lamented that the world situation had deteriorated sharply in the three years since the publication of the first of them. Prospects for the future were alarming: time was short, and every day might count. In 1982, Brandt wrote, 'at a time when other tensions were perhaps even more dangerous than the East-West conflict, $650 billion were spent world-wide on military purposes, adding to an arsenal already capable of destroying humankind many times over'. *Common Security*, the report of the Independent Commission on Disarmament and Security published early in 1982, had pointed out how the burden of expenditure on armaments was exerting a strain on even the wealthiest economies and threatening the stability of states and societies irrespective of their ideology or governmental system. Brandt proposed that interested countries move as soon as possible 'to initiate international economic consultations to prepare the emergency measures for immediate implementation'.[6]

Roundabout 1970, independent of clubs and commissions, James Lovelock developed the idea that earth is a single living organism comparable to the human body, whose organs may be likened to the plants and animals inhabiting the planet. At the suggestion of William Golding, the Nobel prize winning author of *The Lord of the Flies* (1954) and other novels, Lovelock named his all-embracing idea after the Greek goddess Gaia. There were antecedents, as we have seen in earlier chapters. As far back as 1785, for example, at the dawn of the Anthropocene Era, as James Watt was unwittingly accelerating the process of industrial revolution, his friend the geologist James Hutton gave a lecture to the Royal Society of Edinburgh in which he suggested that earth was a 'superorganism', in which the ebb and flow of water to and from the sea along with the interaction of the soil's nutrients with animals and plants were comparable to the circulation of the blood. Lovelock's contribution was to update the concept, bringing together life sciences and earth sciences in a manner reminiscent of Vladimir Vernadsky in 1922. A 'green' commentator, Michael Allaby, optmistically asserted in 1989:

> The old idea, of a world populated by essentially isolated individuals and dominated by conflict, is giving way to a new idea, of the world as a community. As it does so the concept of a living planet where organisms as a whole manage their total environment appears less preposterous than at first it may have seemed. Gaia becomes credible.[7]

In a similar spirit of optimism, after a nuclear arms treaty was signed in 1991 the atomic scientists set the Doomsday Clock at 11:43 p.m., its furthest point ever from midnight. Five years before there had certainly been a powerful reminder of what the unleashing of atomic power might mean, with the meltdown at Chernobyl in April 1986.

History, Historical Sociology, Postmodernism

1968 made a considerable impact on history and other academic disciplines. For example, in the USA, revisionists argued that their own side was largely responsible for the cold war, through abrupt termination in 1945 of the wartime alliance, postwar economic expansionism and global resistance to change.[8]

In 1969, radicals putting forward dissident interpretations of American history were defeated on every front at a business meeting of the American Historical Association, with Eugene D. Genovese denouncing them as 'totalitarians' who should be put down once and for all.[9] One of these, Jesse Lemisch, who had been dismissed from the University of Chicago, officially because his 'political concerns interfered with his scholarship', insisted that it was not so much a political position as dissent from established views that cost him his job and aroused objections to radical history.[10]

To a considerable extent, 1968 meant a change of left-wing focus from class to race and gender. However, in Peter Novick's view, 'no work in European history ever so profoundly and so rapidly influenced so many American historians' as E. P. Thompson's *The Making of the English Working Class*, which was first published in 1964 but took a few years to establish itself as a subtle reinterpretation of the Marxist concept of class. Of course there was no consensus, Novick observing that: 'The founding fathers of the American historical discipline had grounded objectivity in a program of universalism versus particularism, nationalism versus localism, and professionalized versus amateur history. By the 1980s all of the elements of this program had become problematic.'[11]

In the UK, E. P. Thompson was most celebrated for his political activity, but not as an agitator on behalf of the working class, rather as a proponent of the arguments of the Campaign for Nuclear Disarmament (CND) and its fellow organisation European Nuclear Disarmament (END). In such pamphlets as *Protest and Survive* (1980) and *Beyond the Cold War* (1982), Thompson set out a powerful case in the difficult circumstances following the Soviet invasion of Afghanistan in 1979. However, Thompson made little or no attempt to link his work for the CND and END with *The Making of the English Working Class* and his other scholarly publications. Indeed, with the formation of anti-nuclear organisations, Thompson wrote, 'historians had a bit of a problem because, unless they were post-Hiroshima, there really wasn't very much history that historians could actually contribute...because under the criticism of this shadow of nuclear war, all talk of history and culture becomes empty'. On his scholarly approach, he observed that beyond the circuit of capital 'historical materialism (as assumed as hypothesis by Marx, and as subsequently developed in our practice) must be concerned with other "circuits" also: the circuits of power, of the reproduction of ideology, etc., and these belong to a different logic and to other categories.'[12] Generally speaking, British Marxist historians showed more interest in the transition to capitalism than that to socialism. In his outstanding work *Lineages of the Absolutist State* (1974), Perry Anderson addressed 'the historical specificity of European society before the advent of industrial capitalism'. But, as well as criticising contemporary Western Marxism for too little internationalism and too much esotericism, he also suggested that 'the French Revolt of May 1968 marked...a profound historical turning-point'.[13]

In the USSR, 1968 did not make the same public impact as elsewhere. In 1972, P. V. Volobuev was removed from his post as director of the Institute of the History of the USSR of the Academy of Sciences for allegedly exaggerating the element of 'spontaneity' in the Russian Revolution. Access to archives on the Soviet period was restricted, and there were some subjects such as collectivisation, the purges and the 'Great Patriotic War' that had to be interpreted with great care. After the arrival of Gorbachev, historians were slower to take advantage of new opportunities than writers. From 1986, however, as rector of the State Historical Archive Institute, and although a specialist on the French journal *Annales* (or perhaps because of this), Yuri Afanasev encouraged the open discussion of 'blank spots' and called for a full *perestroika* in historical studies. Writing in 1989, R. W. Davies observed that

> *perestroika* is returning not to the Lenin of NEP or the Civil War, but to the Lenin of 1917. In terms of ideas, though not yet of practical achievements, Gorbachev was not being entirely fanciful when he called upon another country and another revolution for the antecedents of *perestroika*.

Referring to the Paris Commune of 1871, he assured a delegation from France: 'If you are looking for the roots of our *perestroika*, you can go back to the French Revolution, and then to the Commune.' He could perhaps have added that its roots can also be found in Adam Smith's *Wealth of Nations*.[14]

Before 1991, however, Marxism-Leninism may have been subject to serious criticism, but it was not completely disestablished, nor the free market given free rein in its stead.

In France, as far as the journal *Annales* was concerned, Peter Burke has noted that a third phase in the journal's development opened around 1968, a phase which was 'marked by fragmentation', retreating from the great questions towards the topic of micro-history. In 1982, Fernand Braudel complained that the heretical, ground-breaking thought of Bloch and Febvre was no longer alive, and that *Annales* had become an established, orthodox journal 'which favours careers and social successes'. In 1981, making clear his attitude to Marx, Braudel pointed out how *Annales* in earlier days had attempted to understand and not denigrate Marxism, and how British Marxists had found the journal a breath of fresh air. His own work on the Mediterranean, including the concept of the *longue durée*, owed a considerable amount to the economic and social analysis of Marxism, if not to its political aspects. In his later work, however, he found himself differing with Marx about the dating of the roots of capitalism. Moreover, it was necessary to recognise that *Capital* was based on the British Industrial Revolution and that the world had completely changed from 1867 when its first volume was published. Nevertheless, Marxism continued to be of use in the study of history, and demanded respect.[15]

Braudel's publications, especially concerning the Mediterranean, continued to exert wide influence. In *Historical Sociology* by Philip Abrams, posthumously published in 1982, the author argues that sociology comprises three types of concern: 1) the transition to industrialism, and its subsequent transformation; 2) the pattern of freedom and constraint involved in the life-histories of individuals in the immediate personal worlds of everyday social life; 3) the relation of the individual as an agent with purposes, expectations and motives to society as a constraining environment of institutions, values and norms. Abrams asserts, with his own italics: 'Doing justice to the reality of history is not a matter of noting the way in which the past provides a background to the present; it is a matter of treating what people do in the present as a struggle to create a future *out of* the past...' After his discussion of Marx, Weber and others, along with his own distinctive contribution, Abrams comes to the conclusion that the way to an effective analytical historical sociology is to be found in works such as Braudel's *The Mediterranean*. However, he is unhappy with Braudel's appropriation of the idea of structure for the very long term, preferring 'to think of epochs, periods and moments as *all* interacting orders of structuring'.[16]

Braudel's masterpiece, we need to recall, was first published in 1949. Moreover, it is not the most approachable of books. Dennis Smith asserts: '*The Mediterranean* is exhilarating and exasperating. The first part is a marvellous journey... By contrast, the second part is intriguing but confusing... Finally, part three of *The Mediterranean* is thoroughly boring and almost unreadable'.[17] Possibly, therefore, the attraction of Braudel's work lies more in his method (structure, conjuncture and event) than in his execution. Certainly, his influence has been great, not least on K. N. Chaudhuri in his book *Asia before Europe* (1990), which includes Braudel's *Material Civilisation* (1967–79) along with *The Mediterranean* in his assertion that to criticise these works on matters of fact or interpretation is 'rather like standing in front of Michelangelo's statue of David...or staring up at his paintings in the Sistine Chapel...and saying that the artist's grasp of the human anatomy was all wrong'.[18]

Immanuel Wallerstein took his homage to the point of becoming head of the Fernand Braudel Center for the Study of Economies, Historical Systems and Civilization. He was also inspired by his reading of Karl Marx and by his practical experience in postcolonial Africa.

In his multivolume *The Modern World-System*, published in 1974, 1980 and 1989, Wallerstein finds the origins of the world-system in early modern Europe, between approximately 1450–1640. The subtitle of the second volume, dedicated to Fernand Braudel, is *Mercantilism and the Consolidation of the European World-Economy, 1600–1750*. Wallerstein goes somewhat beyond 1750 to make the following assertion: 'The Treaty of Paris of 1763 marked Britain's definitive achievement of superiority in…a century-long struggle for the eventual succession to the Dutch hegemony of the mid-seventeenth century'. (1763, let us recall, is the starting date for this book for reasons given in chapter 2, and which are given emphasis by Wallerstein's arguments.) Wallerstein finds the reasons for this victory 'of certain segments of the world bourgeoisie' in the comparative success of British agriculture, commerce and industry, and the comparative stability of British society and government. But Western Europe as a whole was the industrialising core of the process of the development of the world-system, with a dependent periphery supplying raw materials and cheap food and labour and a semi-periphery occupying an intermediate position. Core, periphery and semi-periphery fluctuated from century to century.[19]

At the other end of the interpretive spectrum to historical sociology is postmodernism. Wider use of the concept was developed from the late 1960s onwards in France by, among others, Jacques Derrida, Michel Foucault and Jean-François Lyotard. Essentially, postmodernism was an attack on what were perceived to be concepts imposed from above, in particular of metanarrative and hegemony. A society that was globalised but also decentralised needed to break traditional frameworks of genre, structure and style, the argument ran. Following Ferdinand de Saussure and other authorities, special attention was paid to language itself, to discourse and semiotics. Postmodernism is often used interchangeably if erroneously with another term, postmodernity, which refers primarily to a period of history, beginning in the 1950s but reaching a climax in 1968, in which a reevaluation occurred, as Wallerstein argued, of the world system.

Clearly, the implications of postmodernism for the study of history were serious, even disastrous. The loss of metanarrative had serious implications for its most fundamental characteristic, movement through time, while without some concept of hegemony the presentation of the subject loses shape. On the other hand, by definition, the postmodern approach could not present any complete picture but only fragments. To take again a book often advanced as a seminal influence on the postmodernist approach, Hayden White's *Metahistory*, first published in 1973, argues that 'the best grounds for choosing one perspective on history rather than another are ultimately aesthetic or moral rather than epistemological' and that 'the demand for the scientization of history represents only the statement of a preference for a specific modality of historical conceptualisation'.[20] Adoption of this approach would certainly mean farewell to the historical approach begun in the Scottish Enlightenment. Nevertheless, so many brilliant minds have applied themselves to aspects of postmodernism that it would be foolish not to take at least some of them seriously, especially in view of the arrival of new information technologies and modes of communication.

In 1988, a history book that was neither historical sociology nor postmodernism (although much nearer to the former) not only entered the best seller lists in the USA, but even became an item in the menu of in-flight entertainment during transatlantic air crossings. The book was Paul Kennedy's *The Rise and Fall of the Great Powers: Economic Change and Military Conflict from 1500 to 2000*. Its basic argument is simple enough; in Kennedy's own words and italics: 'The historical record suggests that there is a very clear connection *in the long run* between an individual Great Power's economic rise and fall and its growth and decline as an important power (or world empire).' These two developments do not occur in parallel, Kennedy points out, but there is a tendency for military overspending to accelerate a great power's relative loss of status. His second general suggestion is that 'there is a very strong correlation between the eventual outcome of the *major coalition wars* for European or global mastery, and the amount of productive resources mobilized by each side'.[21] *The Rise and Fall of the Great Powers* is a well-researched and clearly organised work, based on a wide range of sources. However, what attracted so much attention was not the rise and fall of the Habsburg Empire in the sixteenth and seventeenth centuries, nor the rise and fall of the British Empire in the nineteenth and twentieth, but the implications for the USA with the approach of the year 2000. The most discussed chapter was the last – 'To the Twenty-First Century'.

In this chapter, Kennedy considered 'The United States: The Problem of Number One in Relative Decline.' He argued that 'imperial overstretch' threatened the USA, and that, in 1988, 'decision-makers in Washington must face the awkward and enduring fact that the sum total of the United States' global interests and obligations is nowadays far larger than the country's power to defend them simultaneously'. The USA had roughly the same massive array of military obligations across the globe as it had a quarter-century earlier, 'when its shares of world GNP, manufacturing production, military spending, and armed forces personnel were so much larger than they are now'. Relative decline showed not only in agriculture and older manufacturing but also in industrial-technological output. There were also 'unprecedented turbulences in the nation's finances'. Not to look further a quarter-century back, what would be the situation a further 25 years on?[22]

The World by 1991

In the USA, President George Bush spoke in his State of the Union address at the end of January 1991 of 'a new world order – where diverse nations are drawn together in common cause, to achieve the universal aspirations of mankind: peace and security, freedom and the rule of law'. To repel lawless aggression threatening this new world order, an international coalition against the Iraqi dictator Saddam Hussein had been formed consisting of the forces of 28 nations from 6 continents bound together by 12 resolutions of the United Nations. The end of the cold war had been a victory for all humanity, and Europe had become whole and free. Democratic ideas had triumphed in Latin America, too, while the Soviet Union had withdrawn from Afghanistan. But most Americans knew instinctively that 'we had to stop Saddam now, not later. They know that this brutal dictator will do anything, will use any weapon, will commit any outrage, no matter how many innocents suffer. They know we must make sure that control of the world's oil resources does not fall into his hands, only to finance further aggression.' George Bush predicted: 'We will succeed in the Gulf. And when we do, the world community will have sent an enduring warning to any dictator or despot, present or future, who contemplates outlaw aggression.'[23] 'Operation Desert Storm' was launched on 27 February, and deemed to be satisfactorily completed soon afterwards. By the end of the year, however, Bush's vision of 'a new world order' did not appear to be clear, especially since Saddam Hussein was still in power in Iraq, while in Europe some of the excitement and hope aroused by the fall of the Berlin Wall was already dying down. Nevertheless, the collapse of the Soviet Union at the end of the year along with an outbreak of civil disobedience in China reinforced the belief that a new era was dawning.

While it would be wrong to attribute responsibility for the events in Eastern Europe and the wider world to one man or one movement, there can be little doubt that at least some of their origins must be found in the *perestroika* and *glasnost* made famous by the last Soviet leader, President Mikhail Gorbachev. Meetings with President Ronald Reagan, who had formerly deemed the Soviet Union to be the 'evil empire', made a vast contribution to the apparent end of the cold war. A 'Moscow Spring' helped to bring a thaw to what at times had looked like frozen immobility throughout the whole Soviet bloc. The climax came in East Germany, the GDR, early in October 1989 when Gorbachev criticised the government for its failure to reform, while insisting that decisions about its future must be taken in Berlin. After massive demonstrations, the GDR government resigned in November, the Berlin Wall was dismantled and the path opened up towards German reunification. Popular movements throughout the crumbling Soviet bloc continued up to the end of one of the most remarkable years in world history.

By the summer of 1991, the process of change was completed nearly everywhere in the European socialist camp, peacefully for the most part, with dissident Yugoslavia collapsing in an exceptional civil war. Then, the extraordinary movement spread to the Soviet Union itself, as the fate of its most important newspaper illustrated. *Pravda* means both truth and justice: although there were many Soviet citizens who found neither quality in its pages, it was examined carefully every day for nuances in Party policy that could affect the lives of all. Until the end of August, its masthead proclaimed that the newspaper had been founded on 5 May 1912 by V. I. Lenin to become the organ of what would become the Central Committee of the Communist Party of the Soviet Union (CPSU). There was a picture of Lenin and the slogan from the *Communist Manifesto*, 'Proletarians of all countries, unite!'

Then, *Pravda* went through a crisis that ended in a major revision, deeply affecting the status of the man who was the founding father not only of a newspaper, but also of the whole of the Soviet system with the CPSU at its centre. After the failure of a State Committee of an

Extraordinary Situation (SCES) to carry out a coup alleging that the Soviet president Mikhail Gorbachev was ill and unable to carry out his duties, Gorbachev was effectively removed from power anyway by the subsequent Russian president Boris Yeltsin. On 22 August, along with announcements from the president of the USSR and the secretariat of the Central Committee of the USSR, *Pravda*'s front page also gave prominence to an article entitled 'Russia saves the Union', reporting the further speeches and actions of the president of the Russian Federation.

From 24 to 30 August, *Pravda* was not published following an order from the Russian president Yeltsin. Then came the great transformation. On 31 August, the picture of Lenin and the slogan calling on the proletarians of all countries to unite were conspicuous by their absence, and the foundation of the newspaper was declared to be 'at the initiative of V. I. Lenin' rather than by him. Deprived of its former governmental funding, *Pravda* now had to seek financial support from its Russian readers in addition to well-wishers in Italy. By the end of August, then, the Soviet Communist Party's newspaper had suffered complete disestablishment.

On his return to Moscow, Gorbachev presided over little more than the disintegration of the USSR, while Yeltsin and others were far from fully successful in their attempt to set up a Commonwealth of Independent States, as Lithuania, Latvia and Estonia by the Baltic Sea and Georgia by the Black Sea seceded.

Lenin's position was less clear. In the new pluralist circumstances, he remained in his mausoleum on Red Square, maintained at considerable state expense. Some of his statues were taken down, some were damaged but others were left intact. There was still a Communist Party owing allegiance to his ideas, if not as religiously as before. In general, his historical reputation remains a matter of debate. So does that of Chairman Mao, perhaps, although the official conservation of communism in China inhibited public discussion.

After the flag-waving and cheers of the discoverers of freedom, the peoples of the former Soviet Union, and of the former satellites and neighbours, were to realise the limitations placed on that freedom by shortages and inflation, even to the point that some of them would talk of the 'good old days' before 1989. However, the whole continent of Europe was more interdependent than ever before, and more closely interactive with the rest of the world.

Conclusion

Who were the outstanding individuals of the period 1968–1991? At the time of their meeting in Reykjavik in 1986, it seemed that there could be no more than two candidates for the accolade, Ronald Reagan and Mikhail Gorbachev, who momentarily agreed that nuclear weapons should be completely abolished. Yet much of the excitement of that moment has been lost, and the reputation of these two statesmen has fallen some way from its high point. To some extent, this might be because of a growing realisation that 'great men' in general did not dominate the affairs of mankind as much as had been traditionally believed.

The revolution of 1968, comparatively peaceful though considerably provoked by the Vietnam War, encouraged a vigorous debate about the world's future. Many historians were among those who reconsidered their approach to their academic work. However, perhaps the most vigorous school of interpretation of the succeeding period was the postmodernist, which threatened to undermine completely the traditional approach to the subject. Moreover, ingenious and stimulating though much of the new writing was on such subjects as the Third Industrial Revolution, post-industrial society in general and the spread of consumerism in particular, it was ultimately irresponsible in neglecting the fundamental questions facing humankind: the possibility of nuclear war and, increasingly, of ecological disaster.

Chapter 8

MINUTES TO MIDNIGHT, 1991–

The Crisis

In 1991, the Doomsday Clock reached a point far from midnight when a new global nuclear arms treaty was signed – 17 minutes. In 2002, however, a few months after 9/11 and the USA's withdrawal from the Anti-Ballistic Missile Treaty, it advanced a full 10 minutes. Then, in 2007, it moved forwards again to 5 minutes before the fateful hour.[1]

Sixty years after the hands of the Doomsday Clock were first set by a group of atomic scientists the threat of climate change was brought into their calculations. They called the threat of global warming a 'second nuclear age', asserting that the dangers posed by climate change were 'nearly as dire as those posed by nuclear weapons'. They continued: 'The effects may be less dramatic in the short term than the destruction that could be wrought by nuclear explosions, but over the next three to four decades climate change could cause irremediable harm to the habitats upon which human societies depend for survival.' They concluded: 'Not since the first atomic bombs has the world faced such perilous choices'.[2]

Early in 2007, a group of American politicians previously supportive of nuclear weapons – Henry A. Kissinger, Sam Nunn, William J. Perry and George P. Shultz – endorsed the Reykjavik vision shared by presidents Gorbachev and Reagan for a nuclear-free world, asserting:

> Nuclear weapons were essential to maintaining international security during the Cold War because they were a means of deterrence. The end of the Cold War made the doctrine of mutual Soviet-American deterrence obsolete. Deterrence continues to be a relevant consideration for many states with regard to threats from other states. But reliance on nuclear weapons for this purpose is becoming increasingly hazardous and decreasingly effective.

North Korea's recent nuclear test and Iran's refusal to stop its program to enrich uranium – potentially to weapons grade – highlight the fact that the world is now on the precipice of a new and dangerous nuclear era. Most alarmingly, the likelihood that non-state terrorists will get their hands on nuclear weaponry is increasing. In today's war waged on world order by terrorists, nuclear weapons are the ultimate means of mass devastation. And non-state terrorist groups with nuclear weapons are conceptually outside the bonds of a deterrent strategy and present new security challenges.

'The United States and the Soviet Union learned from mistakes that were less than fatal', Kissinger, Nunn, Perry and Shultz continued, asking 'Will new nuclear nations and the world be as fortunate in the next 50 years as we were during the Cold War?' In January 2008, they renewed their appeal for a nuclear-free world, pointing out the special responsibility of the USA and Russia in possessing 95 per cent of the world's nuclear warheads between them, but insisting that other nations must join them in the great endeavour.[3]

An international report, *Climate Change 2007*, went further than The Club of Rome and the Brandt Commission. 'Warming of the climate system is unequivocal', it declared, as was 'evident from observations of increases in global average air and ocean temperatures, widespread melting of snow and ice, and rising global average sea level'. Of the previous 12 years (1995–2006), 11 had ranked among the 12 warmest years since 1850 according to the instrumental record of global surface temperature. Global anthropogenic greenhouse gas emissions had increased by 70 per cent between 1970 and 2004. It was *very likely* that the gases had caused most of the warming since the middle of the twentieth century, and *likely* that the warming over the previous three decades had 'a discernible influence at the global scale on observed changes in many physical and biological systems'. There was *high agreement* and *much evidence* that global greenhouse gas emissions would continue to grow over the next few decades. Even if they were stabilised, anthropogenic warming and sea level rise would continue for centuries. There was *high confidence* that neither adaptation nor mitigation alone could avoid all the impacts of climate change, some of which could be abrupt or irreversible. However, they could complement each other and together significantly reduce the risks of climate change.[4]

In 2010, let us recall, the Doomsday Clock was moved back from five to six minutes before the fatal hour, the reasons given being advances in nuclear and environmental control. We can only hope that the confidence of the atomic scientists was justified and will continue to grow.

What Crisis? 'The End of History', 'The Clash of Civilizations' and After

In the USA, there was celebration of the fall of its rival superpower, the Soviet Union, and of Marxism-Leninism. Now it was possible for John Lewis Gaddis to exonerate us all in 1997 with his assertion that it was 'clear that there was going to be a Cold War whatever the west did'. He continued: 'Who then was responsible? The answer, I think, is authoritarianism in general, and Stalin in particular.' In 2000, recalling President Reagan's denunciation of the 'evil empire', he chided cold war scholars for resisting moral distinctions: 'It isn't "scientific", we tell ourselves; it risks introducing bias into our work; it might lead to smugness, complacency, even triumphalist self-congratulation'.[5]

Francis Fukuyama's *The End of History and the Last Man* was published in 1992, elaborating an argument first put forward in 1989. Appropriately enough, the work was addressed primarily to American readers. Beginning with the observation that the twentieth century 'has made all of us into deep historical pessimists', Fukuyama goes on to make clear what he means by 'all of us': 'As individuals, we can of course be optimistic concerning our personal prospects for health and happiness. By long-standing tradition, Americans as people are said to be continually hopeful about the future.' Having made some acknowledgement of widespread fear and apprehension, Fukuyama proceeds to adhere to the long-standing tradition, announcing that 'good news has come' in the shape of victory for liberalism, that is to say for democracy and the free market. In this manner, his book is infused with the same spirit that may be detected in some of the latter-day historiography in the USA on the cold war.

By history, Fukuyama means 'a single, coherent, evolutionary process, when taking into account the experience of all peoples in all times'. Here, he follows Hegel, who found the end of that process in the liberal state, rather than Marx, who asserted that it would be found in a communist society. For Hegel, man emerged from the master-slave relationship with the French Revolution, to which Fukuyama adds the American. However, as far as the Bolshevik and Chinese revolutions were concerned, 'their only lasting effect would be to spread the already established principles of liberty and equality to formerly backward and oppressed peoples, and to force those countries of the developed world already living in accordance with those principles to implement them more completely'. In other words, whatever their original aims, the Russian and Chinese revolutions served ultimately to advance the cause of their French and American predecessors.[6]

Twenty historians of different persuasions immediately made succinct responses to Fukuyama's arguments in the journal *History Today*, addressing in particular the future viability of Marxism. Two senior British historians were confident: Christopher Hill asserted that Clio has many mansions and recalled John Milton's declaration that truth may have more shapes than one; V. G. Kiernan concluded that 'Human survival will depend on clear thinking and resolute action, to which Marxism, revived by remedying of past shortcomings, should be able to make a contribution second to none.' Other contributors made a range of suggestions: that Tocqueville also deserved serious re-examination; that Marx might still have some relevance to the analysis of the Third World and gender, of British and Russian history; and, on the other hand, that 'to speak of the end of Marxism – as a coherent, believable truth, as a working system, and as a religious faith for any but the incurably short-sighted – is now clearly justifiable' and that there are some 'for whom an eclectic scepticism is now the only order of the day'.[7] Surprisingly, there is almost no reference to the possibility of ecological disaster in the commentaries on Fukuyama's book.

Fukuyama himself does consider 'some cataclysm, either a global nuclear war or an environmental collapse which, despite our best efforts, attacks the physical basis for contemporary human life'. Moreover, if war does not trigger nuclear winter, there might still be 'major environmental consequences that would make the military catastrophe merge with an ecological one'. This could lead to widespread aversion to science, as could an 'ecological catastrophe such as the melting of the ice caps or the desertification of North America and Europe through global warming'. Nevertheless, Fukuyama believes, 'even these extreme circumstances would appear unlikely to break the grip of technology over human civilization, and science's ability to replicate itself'.[8]

'Human civilization' is anatomised in another widely-celebrated book, Samuel P. Huntington's *The Clash of Civilizations and the Remaking of World Order* (1996). No doubt it would be an over-simplification to say that Fukuyama's triumphalist global interpretation of 1992 had been replaced by an apprehensively fragmented approach in 1996. Nevertheless, there is a marked difference of mood from one book to the other, noted by Huntington himself. For him, Fukuyama's basic assumption was that 'the end of the Cold War meant the end of significant conflict in global politics and the emergence of one relatively harmonious world'. But this was put forward in a 'moment of euphoria', which could not last any more than similar moments after the two World Wars. And so, Huntington observes, 'the one harmonious world paradigm is clearly too divorced from reality to be a useful guide to the post-Cold War world'.

In its place, Huntington offers the central theme that 'culture and cultural identities, which at their broadest level are civilization identities, are shaping the patterns of cohesion, disintegration, and conflict in the post-Cold War world'. For Huntington, the West is in decline, while Asian civilisations are on the rise economically, politically and militarily, and Muslim civilisations are expanding demographically. In an emergent world order based on civilisations:

> The survival of the West depends on Americans reaffirming their Western identity and Westerners accepting their civilization as unique not universal and uniting to renew and preserve it against challenges from non-Western societies. Avoidance of a global war of civilizations depends on world leaders accepting and cooperating to maintain the multicivilizational character of global politics.

More strategic considerations are also necessary, in Huntington's view. For example, 'In due course, U.S. Policy will shift from countering proliferation to accommodating proliferation and, if the government can escape from its Cold War mind-set, to how promoting proliferation can serve U.S. and Western interests.' As far as the threat of Chinese hegemony is concerned: 'The greatest danger is that the United States will make no clear choice and stumble into a war without considering carefully whether that is in its national interest and without being prepared to wage such a war effectively.' At the end, as well as here,

Huntington is not a million miles away from Fukuyama's beginning in paying special attention to the USA. While Fukuyama makes some brief mention of the possibility of ecological disaster in his major work, however, Huntington ignores it completely in his.[9]

These two authors are among many downplaying or ignoring the crisis indicated by the Doomsday Clock. But there is no end of history – yet at least, and more to it than the clash of civilisations, as is being increasingly recognised. Indeed, there have been many works tackling the crisis as a whole or aspects of it. As far as the study of history in particular is concerned, Clive Ponting's *A Green History of the World* (1991) and John McNeill's *Something New under the Sun* (2000) are among those deserving special mention. The Forum for the Study of Crisis in the 21st Century was launched in 2008 with 'Rescue! History: A Manifesto for the Humanities in the Age of Climate Change: An Appeal for Collaborators'. A book, *History at the End of the World?*, followed in 2010.[10]

And, *pace* Fukuyama, Marxism is far from dead. István Mészáros reminds us that Karl Marx was fully aware of problems of pollution when he wrote of how freshwater fish were to suffer 'as soon as the river is made to serve industry, as soon as it is polluted by dyes and other waste products and navigated by steamboats, or as soon as its water is diverted into canals'. Concentrating – albeit not exclusively – on economic aspects of the crisis, Mészáros argues for a radical transformation to be brought about by a mass party of the working class.[11] But where is the working class to be found today? For his part, in answer to a question on routes out of the current crisis, David Harvey asserts: 'We are beginning to get a populist outrage, which could produce something equivalent to political movements that have emerged in Latin America'.[12] Arguably, however, the masses in the West, Marx's primary focus, have become consumers wedded to capitalism, more than content to accept its need for continual growth. Perhaps, therefore, even though consumer appetites are evident in Asia too, the proletariat is now rather to be found there. In such a case, it is possible to envisage a syncretic development of Marxism drawing on the age-old, pre-industrial philosophy of the East.

Summary: The Anthropocene Era

Minutes to Midnight, then, joins a growing movement. Its distinctive contribution is to tell the story of the Anthropocene Era since 1763 in conjunction with the development of natural science and the study of history during the same period. Before we reach our conclusion, arguing for a pandisciplinary approach to the present crisis, let us attempt a summary.

In the late eighteenth century, the Anthropocene Era began with the early atmospheric concentration of several greenhouse gases. Scientific advancements accompanying industrial revolution led to the creation and use of the atomic bomb in 1945, giving rise to the creation of the Doomsday Clock in 1947. In 2007, the setting of the Doomsday Clock added climate-changing technologies to the nuclear threat.

We have not presumed to examine in detail these and other scientific phenomena. Rather, we have attempted to throw some light on two themes: the narrative of history since the onset of the Anthropocene Era; and the manner in which historians and other investigators have reacted to this narrative. In other words, we have looked at history in both interconnected senses: the past, and the consideration of the past.

The argument about what happened and how it was analysed may be summarised as follows. The beginning of the Anthropocene Era in the late eighteenth century signalled the interaction of human activity with geological development, bringing together two orders of time, aeons and centuries. The main reason for the conjuncture was the onset of the Industrial Revolution of coal and iron, set in motion by the steam engine perfected by James Watt. The context of Watt's technological activity included the thought of Adam Smith, who advocated economic enterprise, but opposed unrestrained competition, also expressing a strong preference for agriculture in his discussion of the stadial development of human society. The basic narrative of the late eighteenth century has to include the American Revolution, whose spirit was embodied by Thomas Jefferson, and the French Revolution, which led to the emergence of Napoleon Bonaparte.

Bonapartism became an influential phenomenon along with several other -isms taking shape during the first two-thirds of the nineteenth century. Some of them, unfortunately, did not advance the cause of human understanding, in the sense that they marked a departure from the reason and universalism of the Enlightenment. Nationalism in particular may have acted as an indispensable cohesive force for many people living within specific boundaries, but it tended to separate these people from those outside, with the encouragement of Romanticism. Even liberalism in nations that had not consolidated themselves – such as Germany – put up walls against 'others'. While socialism was fundamentally comprehensive and cosmopolitan, some of it was communal on a small-scale. Its most complex form, Marxism, developed the stadial concept of human development put forward by Adam Smith and others, adding the stages of bourgeois and proletarian revolution to be followed by the classless society – a logical product for some, an unfounded prediction for others. On a much longer time scale, Charles Darwin set out the concept of natural stadial development in *The Origin of Species*.

In the late nineteenth century, Social Darwinism was widely accepted in the developed European nations and empires as an ideology of the human struggle for survival of the fittest. This was because Europe ruled the world, although two non-European powers, the USA and Japan, joined in the process at the turn of the century. The process was reinforced by the Second Industrial Revolution – of steel and chemicals, oil and electricity, which also increased the rivalry between the great powers as well as between social classes. The consequence of imperial rivalry was the First World War, which, added to internal instability, also helped to produce the Russian Revolution.

Two opposing world-views in the capitalist USA and the socialist USSR, put forward by Wilson and Lenin respectively, were soon to be challenged by varieties of extreme nationalism in Italy, Germany and Japan. International crisis followed in the Great Depression. Just 20 years after the conclusion of the First World War, a second broke out which was more truly global and much more destructive. While the Axis powers were defeated, some of the Allied powers were weakened, and the USA and the USSR emerged as the leading victors, the superpowers. This process was reflected in the discussions of the 'Big Three' – Churchill, Roosevelt and Stalin, then Truman and later Attlee with Stalin.

The use of the A-bomb accelerated the end of the Pacific War, but also soon led towards Mutually Assured Destruction (MAD). With concepts of strategy reaching out into space, the ideas of Mackinder and Mahan respectively concerning land and sea, still appropriate up to 1945, lost some of their relevance during the years of the cold war and decolonisation. The independence of India in 1947 and the Chinese Revolution of 1949 were among further events shrinking the world. The year 1968 led to widespread consideration of the process of globalisation. Then, the collapse of the Soviet Union in 1991 following the loss of its East European empire meant some redistribution of global power, especially in the direction of Asia.

While the totally unprecedented mortal threat of any third world war remained the greatest reason for considering history after 1945 categorically different from history before, there were other considerations justifying this view. These included a Third Industrial Revolution involving computers of more compact size but much greater intricacy than those developed during the Second World War as well as biological engineering beyond the wildest dreams of 1939–1945. Superimposed on the first and second industrial revolutions, this third transformation, accompanied as it was by a steep rise in the world's population, outstripped them in quantity as well as in nature. The unprecedented demand for raw materials meant that some of the world's supplies no longer seemed inexhaustible, while intensive processing led to widespread pollution of the atmosphere threatening disastrous climate change.

There was cultural revolution, too: extension of television and other electronic communications led to the creation of what came to be called the 'global village'. This development also brought problems of heavy bias, with implications of brainwashing as well as 'dumbing down'. So many and complex have been the problems arising from the sweeping changes that have taken place since 1945 that at least one eminent American historian suggested as early as 1978 that people might well find themselves 'looking back with a certain amount of nostalgia, some years hence, to the "good old days" of the cold war, when all the world had to worry about was the prospect of mutual, instantaneous annihilation'.[13]

As far as the study of history in particular is concerned, the essential argument is as follows. During the Enlightenment of the late eighteenth century, Adam Smith and others formulated an approach that allowed for a scientific study of the past, its progress through time by stages and throughout the whole world at different levels of development, although with emphasis on Europe and on agriculture. Then, the -isms of the nineteenth century summarised above culminated in the attempt to produce a 'new history' in Europe and the USA.

In 1923, let us recall, Henri Pirenne asserted that the nineteenth could be called the century of history since it had added diversity to the scientific universal approach established up to and during the eighteenth century. However, he argued that history would become a science to the extent that it adopted for national history the point of view of universal history. He believed that the only way of arriving at the desired destination was via the comparative method. Unfortunately, before Pirenne spoke, the First World War and Russian Revolution had already led to further, deeper fragmentation. Lenin had produced an updated version of Marxism and Woodrow Wilson had expressed a liberal ideal, while Germany, Italy and Japan were soon to produce supernationalist interpretations of the human past. It was difficult to make a coherent response to these vigorous assertions whilst at the same time transcending the traditional, national approaches.

The end of the Second World War appeared briefly to offer fresh opportunities for a 'new history' but these were quickly lost as a strident Marxism-Leninism vied with 'democratic' propaganda in the world struggle of the cold war intensified by decolonisation and the Chinese Revolution. The arrival of postmodernism posed a further challenge to those seeking to advance the scientific study of history. The alleged end of the cold war in 1991 seemed to offer fresh promise but without much fulfilment before the events of 11 September 2001, which produced yet more obstacles.

Conclusion: Towards Pandisciplinarity

In 2004, in his book *Our Final Century: Will Civilisation Survive the Twenty-First Century?*, the cosmologist Martin Rees observed:

> Science is advancing faster than ever, and on a broader front: bio-, cyber- and nanotechnology all offer exhilarating prospects; so does the exploration of space. But there is a dark side: new science can have unintended consequences; it empowers individuals to perpetrate acts of megaterror; even innocent errors could be catastrophic. The 'downside' from twenty-first century technology could be graver and more intractable than the threat of nuclear devastation that we have faced for decades. And human-induced pressures on the global environment may engender higher risks than the age-old hazards of earthquakes, eruptions, and asteroid impacts.[14]

Jonathan Schell is one of those who have made clear the consequences of nuclear war; Bill McKibben, the implications of the degradation of nature.[15] Among the 'human-induced pressures' was a steep rise in the size of the world's population.

At the end as at the beginning, we ourselves will not presume to trespass on unfamiliar territory, except to observe that the coincidence of geological time with historical time at such a critical moment should concentrate the minds of scholars in all disciplines. With the Doomsday Clock standing at six minutes to midnight and many experts predicting the end of life on earth as we know it if human behaviour does not change, there should be incentive enough for historians to attempt to join geologists and colleagues in other sciences, natural, social and humane, in the attempt to save it.

In order to participate fully in this exercise, historians must adopt the scientific approach first advanced during the Enlightenment and evolving although often neglected since. There have been many obstacles, two of them recent: the collapse of 'scientific' Marxism-Leninism has encouraged rejection of the concept of scientific history; and the postmodernist argument against metanarrative has threatened to deprive it of a necessary characteristic. More generally, the objection may be posed that science is deterministic, and that the study of history must allow for alternatives. Here, as elsewhere, the answer itself is historical: the past is indeed determined, with choice located in the present and free will to be found in the future.[16] We know where the choices of yesteryear have led: to say that a decision was taken as an expression of free will adds nothing to our understanding.

The role of the individual is a further problem. It should not be dismissed, but has certainly been exaggerated. The misconception persists, for example, that Hitler and Stalin caused the Second World War. At the very least, the context in which these and other leaders operated needs to be thoroughly examined, and not necessarily in agreement with Lord Acton that great men are almost always bad men.

Let us recapitulate. Scientific history should be rational, global and evolutionary. We need to apply our reason to overcoming individual, local, national, continental or ideological partiality, avoiding praise and condemnation, triumphalist celebration and humiliating self-abasement. Moreover, history's passage through time must be handled with extreme care. The Western post-industrial society and Eastern industrialising society of today differ radically from the pre-industrial society of more than two centuries ago. Therefore, the assertions made by Adam Smith and Adam Ferguson, for instance, must not be treated as timeless axioms, but as part of an evolving intellectual process.

To help point the way forwards, let us recall the arguments advanced by some illustrious scientists. In 1870, James Clerk Maxwell declared that it was a great step forward in science when men started to think about the nature and number of things rather than their goodness or badness. In 1945, J. Robert Oppenheimer suggested that the common bond of humanity should have precedence over democracy in Western thinking. And in 1968, Andrei Sakharov characterised the scientific method as an objective analysis of facts and concepts.

Let us recall, too, the words that the historian Marc Bloch wrote during dark days in 1941: 'the sciences have shown themselves ever more fruitful and, hence, in the long run more practical, in proportion as they deliberately abandon the old anthropocentrism of good and evil'. While recognising that the science of man would always have its peculiar characteristics, Bloch insisted that 'we are far too prone to judge…and are never sufficiently understanding'.[17]

Thus, good and evil, praise and blame, are concepts that must be jettisoned in an understanding of scientific history that is the imperative of the Anthropocene Era as it threatens to come to an end. Certainly, there has been reluctance among historians to take this approach on board, especially in the English-speaking community where linguistic convention has accompanied deep-set tradition. Indeed, there is much to be said for this tradition as asserted by Keith Thomas:

> Humane scholarship is a vital activity, for without it we would quickly relapse into ignorant solipsism, with no knowledge of the past or comprehension of other languages and cultures. We need scholars to resist the annihilation of our intellectual inheritance, to expose myths and to remind us that there are other ways of thinking and acting than those with which we are familiar.[18]

But is 'humane scholarship' enough? From the Enlightenment onwards, as we have noted in the course of this book, there has been a measure of acceptance of history as science, either tacit or explicit, as well as a recognition of the assistance that historians might derive from other sciences direct, for example from psychology and biology, or by analogy, for example from chemistry and physics. This process must be taken further.

Help might be given in the other direction. Roger Smith goes so far as to assert that 'it is possible to envisage history as a form of knowledge bridging the institutional divisions between the natural sciences, social sciences and humanities. We need history in order to understand, in the fullest sense of "to understand", *any* of the forms that knowledge takes'.[19] Certainly, we need to make as much use as possible of history as we contemplate present problems. At the present critical moment, from whatever quarter, we need all the assistance we can get, and it is therefore possible to envisage a pandisciplinary approach to our present predicament. Already in the early seventeenth century, Francis Bacon wrote:

> And generally let this be a rule, that all partitions of knowledges be accepted rather for lines and veins, than for sections and separations; and that the continuance and entireness of knowledge be preserved. For the contrary hereof hath made particular sciences to become barren, shallow, and erroneous; while they have not been nourished and maintained from the common fountain.[20]

It is high time to overcome Bacon's disappointments in order to realise his aspirations. Towards this end, the question is not so much what history is, as how does history constitute a line and a vein in the body of learning. Thus, the approach should be problem-centred rather than subject-centred.

Let us take as a final example the ongoing debate on climate change,[21] pinpointing the paramount importance of the fourth dimension. Obviously, there is no doubt that the debate is informed by the long-range weather patterns established by meteorologists, making use of the work of other natural sciences and going back at least as far as the beginnings of the Anthropocene Era in the late eighteenth century. Undoubtedly, moreover, natural sciences such as computing will look forward.[22] Certainly, the social sciences are needed to explain the process of industrialisation in general as well as the part played in particular by the BRICS (Brazil, Russia, India and China), the USA, the EU and a wide range of states at varying stages of development. The convergence of geological and human time from the end of the eighteenth century assigns a significant task to historians, while speculative ideas and other sources of inspiration have their part to play, too. Let us recall that, of the makers of the atomic bomb, Leo Szilard, J. Robert Oppenheimer and several of their colleagues acknowledged the stimulus that they received from literary sources.[23]

Let us recall again, too, that their successors, the Board of the Bulletin of Atomic Scientists announced at the beginning of 2010 that they had detected in environmental and other meetings 'signs of a growing political will to tackle the two gravest threats to civilization – the terror of nuclear weapons and runaway climate change', sufficient to move the Doomsday Clock back from five to six minutes before the fatal hour. For the first time ever, they asserted, 'industrialized and developing countries alike are pledging to limit climate-changing gas emissions that could render our planet nearly uninhabitable'. And for the first time since atomic bombs were dropped in 1945, they claimed, 'leaders of nuclear weapons states are cooperating to reduce vastly their arsenals and secure all nuclear bomb-making material.' Thus, 'We are poised to bend the arc of history toward a world free of nuclear weapons.'[24]

The custodians of the 'arc of history' have a distinctive part to play in the pandisciplinary approach that is necessary if the Doomsday Clock is to be moved back more minutes from midnight as the complexities of the Anthropocene Era persist. Two final points must be made here. First, the application of history to a pandisciplinary attempt to explain our present predicament does not mean the abandonment of history in its pure form: indeed, to recall the assertion of E. V. Tarle: 'the more powerful, the more *authentic* the generalising thought, the more it needs the erudite and erudition'.[25] Equally, erudition cannot stand by itself, and needs generalising thoughts: scholarship is a beginning, not an end. Secondly, although a certain emphasis must be given to the period since the late eighteenth century when the era began, this should not mean the neglect of earlier times. Indeed, in a real sense, the whole of human history comprises stages in the evolutionary process leading towards today.[26] Therefore, there is a strong case for applying to all periods the assertion of John McNeill: 'Modern history written as if the life-support systems of the planet were stable, present only in the background of human affairs, is not only incomplete but is misleading.'[27]

NOTES

Chapter 1. Introduction: Times and Approaches

1 Quoted in Clive Ponting, *A Green History of the World* (London: Penguin, 1992), 158.

2 John Gribbin, *Science: A History, 1543–2001* (London: Penguin, 2003), 312–15. Hutton's work is put in context by Roy Porter, *The Making of Geology: Earth Science in Britain 1660–1815* (Cambridge: Cambridge University Press, 1977).

3 Kendall E. Bailes, *Science and Culture in an Age of Revolution: V.I. Vernadsky and His Scientific School, 1863–1945* (Bloomington: Indiana University Press, 1990), 189–94.

4 Dave Webb, 'On the Edge of History: the Nuclear Dimension', in Mark Levene, Rob Johnson and Penny Roberts (eds), *History at the End of the World? History, Climate Change and the Possibility of Closure* (Penrith: Humanities-Ebooks, LLP 2010), 166–8.

5 *Bulletin of the Atomic Scientists*, 17 January 2007. Online: http://www.thebulletin. org/content/media-center/announcements/2007/01/17/doomsday-clock-moves-two-minutes-closer-to-midnight (accessed 3 March 2011).

6 *Bulletin of the Atomic Scientists*, 14 January 2010. Online: http://www.thebulletin. org/content/media-center/announcements/2010/01/14/it-6-minutes-to-midnight (accessed 3 March 2011).

7 Paul J. Crutzen and Eugene F. Stoermer, 'The Anthropocene' in the *IGBP* (International Geosphere-Biosphere Programme) *Newsletter* 41, (2000), 17. Online: http://www.igbp.kva.se/documents/resources/NL_41.pdf (accessed 3 March 2011).

8 For a concise overview, see J. R. McNeill and William H. McNeill, *The Human Web: A Bird's Eye View of World History* (New York: Norton, 2003). For a broader context, see Jared Diamond, *Guns, Germs and Steel: A Short History of Everybody for the Last 13,000 Years* (London: Vintage, 2005).

9 J. Arthur Thomson, *Progress of Science in the Century* (The Nineteenth Century Series) (London: W & R Chambers, 1902), 133. In his preface of September 1902, J. Arthur Thomson writes: 'The reader will understand that the absence of any reference to radium and its marvellous properties is due to the fact that the book was printed before the discovery had been made.'

10 Thomas S. Kuhn, *The Structure of Scientific Revolutions* (Chicago: University of Chicago Press, 1970), 17–18.

11 Fernand Braudel, *The Mediterranean and the Mediterranean World in the Age of Philip II*, 2 vols (London: Collins, 1982), I: 16, 21.

12 Arthur Herman, *The Scottish Enlightenment: The Scots' Invention of the Modern World* (London: Fourth Estate, 2003), 61 (author's own italics). Some critics have found Herman's thesis somewhat exaggerated. See also Christopher Fox, Roy Porter and Robert Wokler (eds), *Inventing Human Science: Eighteenth-Century Domains* (Berkeley: University of California Press, 1995).

13 John Tosh, *Why History Matters* (Basingstoke: Palgrave Macmillan, 2008), 9. Tosh is not alone. To the best of my knowledge, there has been little consideration about how historians should react to the present crisis. However Levene et al., *History at the End of the World?* deserves special attention.

14 Gribbin, *Science: A History, 1543–2001*, xix–xx.

15 Ibid., 242, 249. Karl Marx puts Watt's achievement this way: 'The steam engine itself... did not give rise to any revolution. It was on the contrary, the invention of machines that made a revolution in the form of steam engines necessary.' Karl Marx, *Capital*, 2 vols (London: Swan Sonnenschein, Lowey & Co, 1887), II: 370–1.

16 G. V. Plekhanov, *The Role of the Individual in History* (New York: International Publishers, 1967), 59–60, with Plekhanov's own italics. One of the best discussions of the subject remains Sidney Hook, *The Hero in History: A Study in Limitation and Possibility* (New York: Humanities Press, 1950). It includes a critical analysis of the arguments of Plekhanov.

17 Braudel, *The Mediterranean and the Mediterranean World*, I: 13–22, II: 1242–4.

18 This view is placed in a challenging context by Graeme P. Herd, 'International Relations Theory, Catastrophes and the Need for a New Paradigm?' in Nayef Al Rodhan (ed.), *Potential Global Strategic Catastrophes* (Berlin: LIT Verlag, 2008), 21–38.

19 Herbert Butterfield, *The Whig Interpretation of History* (London: Bell & Sons, 1951).

20 Butterfield, *The Englishman and His History* (Cambridge: Cambridge University Press, 1944), 2, 4–5.

21 An excellent survey of this process is Eric Hobsbawm's *The Age of Revolution, 1789–1848* (London: Abacus, 1962).

Chapter 2. Enlightenment and Revolutions, 1763–1815

1 Paul J. Crutzen and Eugene F. Stoermer, 'The Anthropocene' in the *IGBP* (International Geosphere-Biosphere Programme) *Newsletter* 41, (2000), 17. Online: http://www.igbp.kva.se/documents/resources/NL_41.pdf (accessed 3 March 2011). 1764 is a more appropriate date for 'the invention of the steam engine' than 1784. Perhaps this was a misprint.

2 K. N. Chaudhuri, *Asia before Europe: Economy and Civilisation of the Indian Ocean from the Rise of Islam to 1750* (Cambridge: Cambridge University Press, 1990), 387.

3 Ben Marsden, *Watt's Perfect Engine: Steam and the Age of Invention* (Cambridge: Icon, 2002), 32, 46. This text in general provides a good overview of Watt's

career and significance. Eric Robinson is quoted on 'the most important event' on 97–8.

4 Ibid., 84–5, including quotation from James Hutton.

5 See Anthony Cross, *By the Banks of the Neva: Chapters from the Lives and Careers of the British in Eighteenth-Century Russia* (Cambridge: Cambridge University Press, 1997), 258.

6 Marsden, *Watt's Perfect Engine*, 106; Willard Sterne Randall, *Thomas Jefferson: A Life* (New York: Henry Holt, 1993), 416.

7 Adam Smith, *The Theory of Moral Sentiments*, edited by Ryan Patrick Hanley with an introduction by Amartya Sen (London: Penguin, 2009), 1.

8 Adam Smith, *The Wealth of Nations: Books I–III* (ed. Andrew Skinner) (London: Penguin, 1983), 'Introduction', quoting Smith, 17, 31 and 79.

9 Ibid., 307.

10 Adam Smith, *The Wealth of Nations: Books IV–V* (ed. Andrew Skinner) (London: Penguin, 1999), 32. 'Introduction', xvi–xxix, discusses the influence on Smith of Turgot and Quesnay, omitted here for the sake of simplicity.

11 Adam Ferguson, *An Essay on the History of Civil Society* (1767), ed. Duncan Forbes (Edinburgh: Edinburgh University Press 1996), 122. Cromwell's remark recalls Napoleon's – 'on s'engage, et puis on voit' [one begins, then one sees].

12 Michael Dey, *Adam Smith and Adam Ferguson: Philosophy, Economic Change and Class Limitation in 18th Century Scotland* (University of Aberdeen PhD, 1984), 240, 251. Today, perhaps, the invisible hand may be looked on as a variant of chaos theory or complexity.

13 Derek A. Watts, *Cardinal de Retz: The Ambiguities of a Seventeenth-Century Mind* (Oxford: Oxford University Press, 1980), 193–5, including quotations from Retz himself.

14 Ibid., 235–6.

15 See Smith, *The Theory of Moral Sentiments*, 253, 296 for examples of 'the impartial spectator'; Dey, *Adam Smith*, 272–3.

16 Smith, *The Theory of Moral Sentiments*, 182. Robert Burns put the point more succinctly in *To a Louse*: 'O wad some Power the giftie gie us / To see oursels as others see us! / It wad frae mony a blunder free us, / And foolish notion.' Samuel Carr (ed.), *The Complete Illustrated Poems, Songs and Ballads of Robert Burns* (London: Lomond Books, 1996), 142.

17 Ferguson, *An Essay*, 233, 279–80.

18 A particular consideration here is that Ferguson's concept of 'civil society' was distorted after its translation into German, and re-translation into English. See David Allan, *Adam Ferguson* (Aberdeen: AHRC Centre for Irish and Scottish Studies, University of Aberdeen 2006), 144–8.

19 Smith, *The Wealth of Nations: Books I–III*, 465.

20 Ibid., 466, 520. See also 480: 'The cultivation and improvement of the country…must, necessarily be prior to the increase of the town, which furnishes only the means of conveniency and luxury.'

21 Adam Smith, *An Inquiry into the Nature and Causes of the Wealth of Nations*, eds R. H. Campbell and A. S. Skinner, 2 vols (Oxford: Clarendon Press, 1976), I: 21n22 (from an early draft not quoted in Penguin edition).

22 Julian P. Boyd (ed.), *The Papers of Thomas Jefferson*, 3 vols (Princeton: Princeton University Press, 1950), I: 165–6.

23 Jefferson to John Colvin, the editor of the *Republican Advocate* in Fredericktown, Maryland, 20 September 1810, in Adrienne Koch and William Peden (eds), *Life and Selected Writings of Thomas Jefferson* (New York: Random House, 1944), 606–7.

24 Quoted in Drew R. McCoy, *The Elusive Republic: Political Economy in Jeffersonian America* (Chapel Hill: University of North Carolina Press, 1980), 194–5.

25 Ibid., 111–12.

26 Ibid., 148–50.

27 Quoted in Benjamin F. Wright (ed.), *The Federalist* (Cambridge, MA: Harvard University Press, 1966), 141–2, 296–7.

28 M. Betham-Edwards (ed.), *Travels in France by Arthur Young during the Years 1787, 1788, 1789,* (London: Bell, 1890), xxv–xxvii, 134.

29 Quoted in McCoy, *The Elusive Republic*, 190–1, 195, 259.

30 Peter Burke, *Vico* (Oxford: Oxford University Press, 1985), 54–60.

31 Roy Porter, *Enlightenment: Britain and the Creation of the Modern World* (London: Penguin, 2000), 230–2.

32 Edward Gibbon, *The Decline and Fall of the Roman Empire*, an abridgement by D. M. Low, (London: Chatto & Windus, 1960), 526–30, with Gibbon's own italics.

33 Paul Dukes, *World Order in History: Russia and the West* (London: Routledge, 1996), 29–38. Arguably, this is a scientific comparison.

34 Edmund Burke, 'Thoughts on French Affairs', *Works*, 6 vols (Oxford: Oxford University Press, 1907), IV: 347.

35 Goethe quoted by T. C. W. Blanning, *The Culture of Power and the Power of Culture: Old Regime Europe, 1660–1789* (Oxford: Oxford University Press, 2002), 52.

36 Burke, 'Letters', *Works*, VI: 157.

37 Burke, 'Letters on the Proposals for Peace with the Regicide Directory of France', *Works*, VI: 156–7.

38 Frédéric Bluche, *Le Bonapartisme* (Paris: Presses universitaires de France, 1981), 29.

39 Stuart Woolf, 'The Construction of a European World-View in the Revolutionary-Napoleonic Years', *Past and Present* 137 (1992): 100–1.

40 Pieter Geyl, *Napoleon For and Against* (London: Penguin, 1949), 7, 9–10.

Chapter 3. Nations and -Isms, 1815–1871

1 W. Alison Phillips, 'The Congresses, 1815–1822', *Cambridge Modern History*, 12 vols (Cambridge: Cambridge University Press, 1907), X: 1.

2 T. C. W. Blanning, 'Epilogue: The Old Order Transformed, 1789–1815', in Euan Cameron (ed.), *Early Modern Europe: An Oxford History* (Oxford: Oxford University Press, 1999), 372.

3 R. C. Bridges, Paul Dukes, J. D. Hargreaves and William Scott (eds), *Nations and Empires: Documents on the History of Europe and on its Relations with the World since 1648* (London: Macmillan, 1969), 122–6.

4 G. W. F. Hegel, *The Philosophy of History* (Baloche ebook, 2001), 44, 103–4.

5 Bridges et al., *Nations and Empires*, 127–31.

6 I owe this observation to David Saunders.

7 W. O. Henderson, *Friedrich List: Economist and Visionary, 1789–1846* (London: Cass, 1983), 146, 159, 167; Jacques Droz, *Europe between Revolutions, 1815–1848* (Glasgow: Collins, 1967), 55. Regarding the American economy, List might be called a Hamiltonian.

8 Benjamin Constant, *Political Writings* trans. and ed. Biancamaria Fontana (Cambridge: Cambridge Universty Press, 1999), 161, 183.

9 Alexis de Tocqueville, *Democracy in America* (ed. Henry Steele Commager) (London: Oxford University Press, 1955), 57.

10 Mary Warnock, 'Introduction' to John Stuart Mill, *Utilitarianism* (London: Fontana, 1962), 7–31. John Stuart Mill also wrote on the subjection of women.

11 Karl Marx, *The Revolutions of 1848: Political Writing*, vol. 1 (ed. David Fernbach) (Harmondsworth: Penguin, 1973), 22–5, 94–7.

12 Ibid., 67.

13 Ibid., 67, 70–3.

14 Ibid., 74–6, 84–7.

15 Charles Darwin, *The Origin of Species* (ed. J. W. Burrow) (London: Penguin, 1981), 458.

16 A. Desmond and J. Moore, *Darwin* (London: Penguin, 1992), xix.

17 Roy Porter and Mikuláš Teich (eds), in their introduction to *Romanticism in National Context* (Cambridge: Cambridge University Press, 1988), 1–7.

18 Quoted in Edward O. Wilson, *Consilience: The Unity of Knowledge* (London: Little, Brown and Co., 1998), 6–7.

19 Patrick Gardiner (ed.), *Theories of History* (New York: The Free Press, 1959), 73–9.

20 Alfred Henry Huth, *The Life and Writings of Henry Thomas Buckle* 2 vols (London: Sampson Low, Marston, Searle & Rivington, 1880), I: 63–4, 147, 152, 245. Needless to say, Buckle was widely condemned for his assertion of the superiority of intellectual over moral laws in the explanation of history.

21 Eber Jeffery, '"Nothing Left to Invent"', *Journal of the Patent Office Society* 22, no. 7 (1940): 478–81.

22 Quoted in the introduction to *Official Descriptive and Illustrated Catalogue of the Great Exhibition of the Works of Industry of All Nations*, vol. 1 (London, 1851), 3. I owe the reference to Prince Albert's Speech and much else to Nick Fisher.

23 Bridges et al., *Nations and Empires*, 146.

24 Lefebvre quoted in Pieter Geyl, *Debates with Historians* (London: Collins, 1974), 105.

25 Edmund Wilson, *To the Finland Station: A Study in the Writing and Acting of History* (London: Collins, 1962), 10–12, 13, 16, 22–4, 37–8.

26 Owen Dudley Edwards, *Macaulay* (London: Weidenfeld & Nicolson, 1988), 152.

27 Thomas Babington Macaulay, *The History of England from the Accession of James II*, 2 vols (London: Dent, 1907), I: 9–10.

28 J. L. Black, *Nicholas Karamzin and Russian Society in the Nineteenth Century: A Study in Russian and Political Thought* (Toronto: University of Toronto Press, 1975), 58, 100; Richard Pipes, *Karamzin's Memoir on Ancient and Modern Russia: A Translation and an Analysis* (Cambridge, MA: Harvard University Press, 1959), 124.

29 *Encyclopaedia Britannica*, 13th Edition, 3 vols in addition to 11th Edition, 32 vols (London, 1926), III: 307–8; Leopold von Ranke, *The Theory and Practice of History*

(eds George Iggers and Konrad Von Moltke) (Indianapolis: Bobbs Merrill, 1973), 119. Ranke deemed Bancroft an outstanding 'democratic' historian.

30 Hayden White, *Metahistory: The Historical Imagination in Nineteenth-Century Europe* (Baltimore: Johns Hopkins University Press, 1973), 426–7.

31 Karl Marx, 'The Eighteenth Brumaire of Louis Bonaparte', *Selected Works*, 2 vols (London: Lawrence and Wishart, 1942), II: 315.

Chapter 4. Natural Selection, 1871–1921

1 See, for example, Paul Kennedy, 'Mahan versus Mackinder: Two Interpretations of British Sea Power', *Strategy and Diplomacy, 1870–1945* (London: Allen & Unwin, 1983).

2 See the remarkable work by C. A. Bayly, *The Birth of the Modern World, 1780–1914: Global Connections and Comparisons* (Oxford: Blackwell, 2004).

3 Stephen Kern, *The Culture of Time and Space, 1880–1918*, (London: Weidenfeld & Nicolson, 1983), 12–15; Edwin A. Pratt, *The Rise of Rail-Power in War and Conquest* (London: P. S. King, 1915), 356.

4 General F. von Bernhardi, *Germany and the Next War* (London: Edward Arnold, 1914), chapter 5.

5 J. Clerk Maxwell, 'Presidential Address to Section A, British Association', *Nature* 2, (1870): 419–22.

6 Albert Einstein, 'Maxwell's influence on the development of the conception of physical reality' in J. J. Thomson (ed.), *James Clerk Maxwell: A Commemoration Volume* (Cambridge: Cambridge University Press, 1931), 71. Einstein went on to say that the change had not yet been completely carried out.

7 Howard J. Rogers (ed.), *Congress of Arts and Science, Universal Exposition, St. Louis*, 8 vols (Boston: Houghton Mifflin, 1904) II: 3–5.

8 Ibid., II: 19–20, 38–9, 50–1, 184–7. See also Georg G. Iggers and James M. Powell (eds), *Leopold von Ranke: The Shaping of the Historical Discipline* (Syracuse: Syracuse University Press, 1990), 176–9.

9 William M. Sloane, 'History and Democracy', *American Historical Review* 1 (1895–6): 16–17.

10 Karl Lamprecht, *What Is History? Five Lectures on the Modern Science of History* (New York: Macmillan, 1905), 190–227.

11 Henri Berr, *La synthèse en histoire: son rapport avec la synthèse générale* (Paris: Albin Michel, 1953), xi–xvi, 1–3, 222–3.

12 Patrick Gardiner (ed.), *Theories of History* (New York: The Free Press, 1959), 225–6.

13 Paul Dukes, 'Klyuchevsky and the Course of Russian History', in Paul Dukes (ed.), *Russia and Europe* (London: Collins & Brown, 1991), 108–15.

14 Lord Acton [John Emerich Edward Dalberg], *Longitude 30 West: A Confidential Report to the Syndics of the Cambridge University Press* (Cambridge: Cambridge University Press, 1969); James Bryce, 'John Emerich Dalberg-Acton, Lord Acton', *Studies in Contemporary Biography* (London: Macmillan, 1920), 383–94; Gertrude Himmelfarb, 'The American Revolution in the Political Theory of Lord Acton', *Journal of Modern History* 21, no. 4 (1949), including some interesting comparisons between the approaches of Lord Acton and Edmund

Burke; John Nurser, *The Reign of Conscience: Individual, Church and State in Lord Acton's History of Liberty* (London: Garland, 1987), 84–93, 100–5.

15 J. B. Bury, *An Inaugural Lecture* (Cambridge: Cambridge University Press, 1903), 7, 16; *Congress of Arts and Science*, II: 152; Roger Smith, *Being Human: Historical Knowledge and the Creation of Human Nature* (Manchester: Manchester University Press, 2007), chapter 5. The view of history as literature was put most eloquently by G. M. Trevelyan. See below, chapter 5, note 5.

16 Stanley Leathes, 'Modern Europe', XII: 1; G. P. Gooch, 'The Growth of Historical Science', XII: 850; in Stanley Leathes, A. W. Ward and G W. Prothero (eds), *Cambridge Modern History*, 12 vols (Cambridge: Cambridge University Press, 1910).

17 All quotations in this paragraph are from Patrick Brantlinger, 'Mass Media in *fin-de-siècle* Europe' in Mikuláš Teich and Roy Porter (eds) *Fin de siècle and its Legacy* (Cambridge: Cambridge University Press, 1990), 105. Although newspapers were to be found throughout the colonial world, freedom of the press was absent.

18 Hans Rogger, 'Russia in 1914', *Journal of Contemporary History* 1, no. 4 (1996): 95–6.

19 P. N. Miliukov, *Istoriia vtoroi russkoi revoliutsi* (Moskva: Rosspen, 2001), 17.

20 Quoted by Arno J. Mayer, *Political Origins of the New Diplomacy, 1917–1918* (New Haven: Yale University Press, 1970), 393. For an attempt at global analysis in a chronological context see Paul Dukes, *October and the World: Perspectives on the Russian Revolution* (London: Macmillan, 1978).

Chapter 5. From Relativity to Totalitarianism, 1921–1945

1 J. D. Bernal, *Science in History*, 4 vols (London: Penguin, 1969), III: 746.

2 *Congressional Record*, 4 March 1921, 4–6.

3 R. C. Bridges, Paul Dukes, J. D. Hargreaves and William Scott (eds), *Nations and Empires: Documents on the History of Europe and on its Relations with the World since 1648* (London: Macmillan, 1969), 261–4.

4 H. Stuart Hughes, *Oswald Spengler* (New Brunswick, NJ: Transaction, 1992), 9–13.

5 G. M. Trevelyan, 'The Muse of History', *The Recreation of an Historian* (London: Thomas Nelson & Sons, 1919), 8, 40. David Cannadine, *G. M. Trevelyan: A Life in History* (London: Harper Collins, 1993), 226–7, writes: 'like Thucydides, like Gibbon, like Tocqueville, like Macaulay, Trevelyan possessed a mind of remarkable range, power, erudition and creativity' and 'occupies an assured place in Clio's Hall of Fame'.

6 Charles A. Beard, *Crosscurrents in Europe Today* (Boston: Marshall Jones Company, 1922), v, 176–7, 236, 251–2.

7 E. V. Tarle, 'Ocherednaia zadacha', *Annaly: zhurnal vseobshchei istorii* 1, (Peterburg: Petrograd 1922): 6–9, 12–16.

8 Quoted in Clive Ponting, *A Green History of the World* (London: Penguin, 1992), 158. See more generally John Barber, *Soviet Historians in Crisis, 1928–1932* (London: Macmillan, 1981).

9 Henri Pirenne, 'De la méthode comparative en histoire', *Compte Rendu du V Congrès International des Sciences Historiques* (Brussels, 1923), 19–32; RIM, 'Pirenne, Henri', in John Cannon (ed.), *The Mionary of Historians* (Oxford: Blackwell, 1988). See Karl Dietrich Erdmann, *Toward a Global Community of Historians: The International Historical Congresses and the International Committee of Historical Sciences, 1898–2000* (New York and Oxford: Berghahn Books, 2005) for an excellent survey.

10 For example, according to Richard Rhodes, *The Making of the Atomic Bomb* (London: Penguin, 1986), 16, Fritz Haber's 'method for fixing nitrogen from the air to make nitrates for gunpowder saved Germany from early defeat in the Great War'. But John McNeill (*Something New under the Sun: An Environmental History of the Twentieth Century* (London: Penguin, 2000), 24–5) points out that Haber developed nitrates as fertiliser, too – 'he more than anyone else shaped the world's soil chemistry in the twentieth century'.

11 Peter Burke, *The French Historical Revolution: The Annales School, 1929–1989* (Cambridge: Polity, 1990), 2, writes that from the 1920s to 1945, the *Annales* movement was 'small, radical and subversive.'

12 Richard J. Evans, *The Third Reich at War, 1939–1945* (London: Penguin, 2008), 174–5.

13 H. A. L. Fisher, *A History of Europe* (London: Edward Arnold, 1936), v, 1.

14 Charles A. Beard, 'Written History as an Act of Faith', *American Historical Review* 39 (1933–4): 225–9; Charles A. Beard and Alfred Vagts, 'Currents of Thought in Historiography', *American Historical Review* 42, (1936–7): 466–83. Beard's 'Written History as an Act of Faith' makes an interesting comparison with Carl Becker's American Historical Association presidential address of 1931, 'Everyman His Own Historian'. See Peter Novick, *That Noble Dream: The "Objectivity Question" and the American Historical Profession* (Cambridge: Cambridge University Press, 1988), 252–8. Novick comments that no other presidential addresses 'ever occasioned as much discussion'.

15 Novick, *That Noble Dream*, 281, 287.

16 See generally H. L'Etang, *The Pathology of Leadership* (New York: Hawthorn Books, 1970) and David Owen, *In Sickness and in Power: Illness in Heads of Government during the last 100 years* (London: Methuen, 2008). Niall Ferguson (ed.), *Virtual History: Alternatives and Counterfactuals* (London: Macmillan, 1988), contains some challenging essays.

17 Bridges, Dukes and others, *Nations and Empires*, 286–7.

18 See Richard Rhodes, *The Making of the Atomic Bomb*, 565–6.

19 Ibid., 448, 642.

20 David Holloway, *Stalin and the Bomb: The Soviet Union and Atomic Energy, 1939–1956* (London: Yale University Press, 1994), 32–3, 148–9; Kendall E. Bailes, *Science and Russian Culture in an Age of Revolutions: V. I. Vernadsky and His Scientific School, 1863–1945* (Bloomington: Indiana University Press, 1990), 162–3, 194. Vernadsky took the term 'noosphere' from the Jesuit scientist Teilhard de Chardin and the French philosopher Edouard Le Roy.

21 John Gribbin, *Science: A History, 1543–2001* (London: Penguin, 2003), 452–3. 'Independent evidence' came from research into tectonic plates from the 1950s onwards.

22 Rhodes, *The Making of the Atomic Bomb*, 58–60.

23 Ibid., 107–8.

24 Ibid., 123, 150, 205, 446, 572.

Chapter 6. Superpower, 1945–1968

1 Quoted in Richard Rhodes, *The Making of the Atomic Bomb* (London: Penguin, 1986), 749, 760–3, 766–8.

2 Quoted in David Holloway, *Stalin and the Bomb: The Soviet Union and Atomic Energy, 1939–1956* (London: Yale University Press, 1994), 194–5, 337–8.

3 Andrei D. Sakharov, *Progress, Coexistence, and Intellectual Freedom* (London: Andre Deutsch, 1968), 25.

4 *Encyclopaedia Britannica* (13th ed.), 3 vols (London and New York: Encyclopaedia Britannica Company Limited, 1926), III: 681.

5 William T. R. Fox, 'The Super-Powers Then and Now', *International Journal* 35, (1979–80): 417–30.

6 Quoted in Dean Albertson (ed.), *Eisenhower as President* (New York: Hill & Wang, 1963), 162–3.

7 John Gribbin, *Science: A History, 1543–2001*, (London: Penguin, 2003), 563, 569. An essential contribution was made by Rosalind Franklin who died in 1958.

8 Howard K. Smith, *The State of Europe* (London: Cresset Press, 1950), 66–7.

9 R. A. C. Parker, 'British Perceptions of Power: Europe between the Super-powers', in Josef Becker and Franz Knipping (eds), *Power in Europe? Great Britain, France, Italy and Germany in a Postwar World, 1945–1950* (Berlin: W de Gruyter, 1986), 449.

10 Walter LaFeber (ed.), *The Origins of the Cold War, 1941–1947: A Historical Problem with Interpretations and Documents* (New York: John Wiley & Sons, 1971), 70.

11 Quoted in Thomas G. Paterson, *Soviet-American Confrontation: Postwar Reconstruction and the Origins of the Cold War* (London: Johns Hopkins University Press, 1973), 8–9.

12 Earlier uses of the term 'iron curtain' were made by in 1919 by Ethel Snowden, a British visitor to Soviet Russia, the Russian writer V. V. Rozanov, and later in 1945 by the Nazi propagandist Josef Goebbels.

13 LaFeber (ed.), *The Origins of the Cold War*, 155–6.

14 Jawarhalal Nehru, *The Discovery of India* (London: Meridian 1946), 472.

15 E. H. Carr, *What Is History?*, 2nd ed. (London: Penguin, 1987), 40–1.

16 Arthur M. Schlesinger Jr, *The Vital Center: The Politics of Freedom* (Boston: Houghton Mifflin, 1949), 241–2.

17 R. G. Collingwood, *An Autobiography* (Oxford: Oxford University Press, 1970), 79, 87–8, 100, 112, 127–8, 152–3, 167; R. G. Collingwood, *The Idea of History* (Oxford: Oxford University Press, 1961).

18 Stefan Collini, *Absent Minds: Intellectuals in Britain* (Oxford: Oxford University Press, 2006), 331–49, dismisses Collingwood's quest as 'professorial cackling'.

19 Quoted in Patrick Gardiner (ed.), *Theories of History* (New York: The Free Press, 1959), 200–1, 205.

20 *Time*, 17 March 1947.

21 Marc Bloch, *The Historian's Craft* (Manchester: Manchester University Press, 1967), 47, 142–4.

22 Fernand Braudel, *The Mediterranean and the Mediterranean World in the Age of Philip II*, 2 vols (London: Collins, 1975), I: 22.

23 Ibid., II: 1242–4.

24 Ibid., I: 21.

25 Ibid., I: 20, 353.

26 For an attempt to apply Braudelian methodology to the cold war, see Paul Dukes, *The Last Great Game: USA versus USSR: Events, Conjunctures, Structures* (London: Pinter, 1989).

27 Quoted in Ved Mehta, *Fly and the Fly-Bottle: Encounters with British Intellectuals* (London: Penguin, 1965), 104, 145. Collini, *Absent Minds*, 375–92, entitles his section on A. J. P. Taylor 'Nothing to Say'.

28 Christopher Hill, R. H. Hilton and E. J. Hobsbawm, 'Origins and Early Years', *Past and Present* 100 (1983): 3–6.

29 Lawrence Stone, *The Past and the Present Revisited* (London: Routledge & Kegan Paul, 1987), 76.

30 Conyers Read, 'The Social Responsibilities of the Historian', *American Historical Review* 55, no. 2 (1950): 283–4.

31 See notes 1 and 3 above.

32 Walter LaFeber, *America, Russia, and the Cold War, 1945–1996* (New York: McGraw-Hill 1997), 243. LaFeber's outstanding work, first published in 1967, is still going strong.

33 F. R. Dulles, *The Imperial Years* (New York: Thomas Y. Crowell Company, 1956), vii–ix.

34 Eric Hobsbawm, *Age of Extremes: The Short Twentieth Century, 1914–1991* (London: Abacus, 1995), puts the cold war in a stimulating context.

35 K. Shteppa, *Russian Historians and the Soviet State* (New Brunswick: Rutgers University Press, 1962), 326.

36 John Kent, *America, the UN and Decolonisation: Cold War conflict in the Congo* (London: Routledge, 2010), 2. General works on the topic include R. F. Holland, *European Decolonization, 1918–1981: An Introductory Survey* (Basingstoke: Macmillan, 1985) and John D. Hargreaves, *African Decolonisation* (Basingstoke: Macmillan, 1966).

37 Odd Arne Westad, *The Global Cold War: Third World Interventions and the Making of Our Times* (Cambridge: Cambridge University Press, 2007), 143.

38 Jan Romein, 'Theoretical History', *Journal of the History of Ideas* 9, (1948).

39 'The Common Human Pattern: Origin and Scope of Historical Theories', *Journal of World History* 4, (1957–8). Jean-Paul Sartre stressed that what was becoming known as the Third World 'finds *itself* and speaks to *itself* through the voice of Frantz Fanon in *Les damnés de la terre*, first published in Paris 1961. See the translation by Constance Farrington, *The Wretched of the Earth* (London: Penguin, 1967), 9.

40 Carr, *What is History?*, 147–8. The quotation is unchanged from the 1st edition of 1961.

41 E. V. Tarle, 'SSSR – mirovaia derzhava', as in *Sochineniia*, 12 vols (Moscow: Izdatel'stvo Akademii Nauk, 1957–62) XII: 239–48.

42 C. Wright Mills, *The Marxists* (London: Penguin, 1963), 450–6.

43 Perry Anderson, *Considerations on Western Marxism* (London: NLB, 1976), 68, 102, 105, with his own emphasis.

44 Carson and Ward are quoted in Kevin Desmond, *Planet Savers* (Sheffield: Greenleaf, 2008), 118–9, 131–2.

Chapter 7. Planet Earth, 1968–1991

1 See C. A. Bayly's masterful survey, *The Birth of the Modern World, 1780–1914: Global Connections and Comparisons* (Oxford: Blackwell, 2004).

2 Neal Ascherson, 'When hope faded in the streets of the East', *Observer Review*, 20 January 2008.

3 Immanuel Wallerstein, '1968: Revolution in the World-System', *Geopolitics and Geoculture: Essays on the Changing World-System* (Cambridge: Cambridge University Press, 1991), 13–14, 65–83. Wallerstein's italics.

4 Donella H. Meadows, Dennis L. Meadows, Jørgen Randers and William M. Behrens III, *The Limits to Growth: A Report for the Club of Rome's Project on the Predicament of Mankind* (London: Earth Island, 1972), 9–10, 23–4, 186–97.

5 Mihajlo Mesarovic and Eduard Pestel, *Mankind at the Turning Point: The Second Report to the Club of Rome* (London: Hutchinson, 1975), 143–8, with their own italics. Clive Ponting, *A Green History of the World* (London: Penguin, 1992), 402 criticises the Club of Rome for exaggeration of the immediate threat from shortage of resources and energy. But Keith Suter, 'Fair Warning: The Club of Rome Revisited' (1999), declares that 'the warning from the Club of Rome remains valid.' Online: http://www.abc.net.au/science/slab/rome/default.htm (accessed 15 March 2011, originally published on the Club of Rome website).

6 The Brandt Commission, *North-South: A Programme for Survival* (London: Pan, 1980); and *Common Crisis North-South: Co-operation for World Recovery* (London: Pan, 1983), 6, 7. It is noteworthy that neither the Club of Rome nor the Brandt Commission had any member from the Soviet Union. It is also noteworthy that the Club of Rome is still extant, insisting on the continued relevance of its arguments, while the Brandt Commission was disbanded in 1983.

7 Michael Allaby, *Guide to Gaia* (London: Optima, 1989), 110. James Lovelock himself, in *The Vanishing Face of Gaia: A Final Warning* (London: Allen Lane, 2009), sets out a programme for human survival, including the use of nuclear energy.

8 Richard Dean Burns, 'Foreword', in J. L. Black, *Origins, Evolution, and Nature of the Cold War: An annotated Bibliographic Guide* (Oxford: ABC-Clio, 1986), xx.

9 Peter Novick, *That Noble Dream: The "Objectivity Question" and the American Historical Profession* (Cambridge: Cambridge University Press, 1988), 435.

10 Ronald Radosh, 'The Bare-Knuckled Historians', *Nation*, 2 February 1970.

11 Novick, *That Noble Dream*, 440, 521.

12 E. P. Thompson, 'Marxism and History' and 'Agenda for Radical History', in Dorothy Thompson (ed.), *The Essential E. P. Thompson* (New York: The New Press, 2001), 474, 491.

13 Perry Anderson, *Lineages of the Absolutist State* (London: NLB, 1975), 397; *Considerations on Western Marxism* (London: NLB, 1976) 95.

14　R. W. Davies, *Soviet History in the Gorbachev Revolution* (Basingstoke: Macmillan, 1989), 203 (quoting *Pravda*, 30 September 1987).

15　Peter Burke, *The French Historical Revolution: The Annales School, 1929–1980* (Cambridge: Polity, 1990), 2; V. Daline, *Hommes et idées* (Moscow: Progress, 1983), 426–9. I owe this reference to Terry Brotherstone.

16　Philip Abrams, *Historical Sociology* (Shepton Mallett: Open Book, 1982), 7–8, 334–5, with his own italics.

17　Dennis Smith, *The Rise of Historical Sociology* (Cambridge: Polity, 1991), 111–12. Smith's adverse comments do not necessarily spring from his academic specialisation. Some early modernist historians such as Hugh Trevor-Roper and J. H. Hexter have been more negative in their criticism of Braudel's work.

18　K. N. Chaudhuri, *Asia before Europe: Economy and civilisation of the Indian Ocean from the rise of Islam to 1750* (Cambridge: Cambridge University Press, 1990), 6.

19　Immanuel Wallerstein, *The Modern World System II: Mercantilism and the Consolidation of the European World-Economy, 1600–1750* (London: Academic Press, 1980), 257–9, 289. See also Smith, *The Rise*, 96–7. Among those in disagreement with Wallerstein was Andre Gunder Frank, who argued that the world system was formed no later than the fourth millennium BCE.

20　Hayden White, *Metahistory: The Historical Imagination in Nineteenth-Century Europe* (Baltimore: Johns Hopkins University Press, 1973), xii.

21　Paul Kennedy, *The Rise and Fall of the Great Powers: Economic Change and Military Conflict from 1500 to 2000* (London: Unwin Hyman, 1988), xxii–xxiv.

22　Ibid., 515, 521, 525–6. Kennedy duly made his own forecasts in *Preparing for the Twenty-First* Century (London: Harper Collins, 1993).

23　*Congressional Record – Senate*, 29 January 1991, S 1216–19.

Chapter 8.　Minutes to Midnight, 1991–

1　Dave Webb, 'On the Edge of History: the Nuclear Dimension' in Mark Levene, Rob Johnson and Penny Roberts (eds), *History at the End of the World? History, Climate Change and the Possibility of Closure* (Penrith: Humanities eBooks, LLP, 2010), 166–87.

2　*Bulletin of the Atomic Scientists*, 17 January 2007. Online: http://www.thebulletin. org/content/media-center/announcements/2007/01/17/doomsday-clock-moves-two-minutes-closer-to-midnight (accessed 3 March 2011).

3　*Wall Street Journal*, 4 January 2007, 15 January 2008. Kissinger was secretary of state from 1973 to 1977, Nunn was formerly chairman of the Senate Armed Services Committee, Perry secretary of defense from 1994 to 1997 and Shultz secretary of state from 1982 to 1989.

4　*Climate Change 2007: Synthesis Report from Intergovernmental Panel on Climate Change*, Fourth Assessment Report, 1–23, with its own italics. And see note 21 below.

5　John Lewis Gaddis, *We Now Know: Rethinking Cold War History* (Oxford: Oxford University Press, 1997), 294; 'On Starting All Over Again: A Naïve Approach to the Study of the Cold War', in Odd Arne Westad (ed.), *Reviewing the Cold War: Approaches, Interpretations, Theory* (London: Frank Cass, 2000), 36. Gaddis singles out Melvyn Leffler for worrying about triumphalism. See, for example, Leffler's article, 'The Cold War: What Do "We Now Know"?', *American Historical Review* 104, no. 2 (1999).

6 Francis Fukuyama, *The End of History and the Last Man* (London: Penguin, 1992), xiii, 51, 66, 126, 152, 283.

7 Alan Ryan in his introduction to *After the End of History* (London: Collins & Brown, 1992), 29, 47, 97.

8 Fukuyama, *The End of History*, 86–7. In *Our Posthuman Future: Consequences of the Biotechnology Revolution* (London: Profile, 2005), Fukuyama concentrates on the potential threat to liberal democracy posed by this revolution. There is little reference to the danger of nuclear and ecological disaster in Francis Fukuyama, *After the Neocons: America at the Crossroads* (London: Profile, 2006).

9 Samuel P. Huntington, *The Clash of Civilizations and the Remaking of World Order* (New York: Simon & Schuster, 1996), 20–1, 31–2, 164, 192, 232–3, 301–21. There is no more reference to the possibility of ecological disaster in Samuel P. Huntington, *Who Are We? America's Great Debate*, (London: Free Press, 2004).

10 Mark Levene and others, *History at the End of the World?*. See note 1, above.

11 István Mészáros, *The Structural Crisis of Capital* (New York: Monthly Review Press, 2010) 65, 92, 171, 201–2. Also worth viewing is Ronaldo Munck, *Marx @ 2000: Late Marxist Perspectives* (Basingstoke: Macmillan, 2000) especially chapter 2, '"Red and Green": Marxism and Nature', 21–39.

12 Joseph Choonara, 'Interview: David Harvey – Exploring the logic of capital', *Socialist Review*, April 2009, 7. Online: http://www.socialistreview.org.uk/article. php?articlenumber=10801 (accessed 3 March 2011).

13 John Lewis Gaddis, *Russia, the Soviet Union and the United States: An Interpretative History* (New York: Wiley, 1978), 279.

14 Martin Rees, *Our Final Century: Will Civilisation Survive the Twenty-First Century?* (London: Heinemann, 2004), vii. Nick Bostrom and Milan M. Ćirković (eds), *Global Catastrophic Risks* (Oxford: Oxford University Press, 2008) is a wide-ranging collection of essays supplementing the argument put forward by Rees.

15 See Jonathan Schell, *The Fate of the Earth* (London: Picador, 1982); Bill McKibben, *The End of Nature* (London: Penguin, 1990). See also Dave Webb, 'On the Edge of History: the Nuclear Dimension' in Levene and others, *History at the End of World?*. John McNeill, *Something New under the Sun: An Environmental History of the Twentieth Century* (London: Penguin, 2000), and Clive Ponting, *A Green History of the World* (London: Penguin, 1992) both also deserve special attention.

16 See Paul Dukes, *World Order in History: Russia and the West* (London: Routledge, 1996), 143–4.

17 Marc Bloch, *The Historian's Craft* (Manchester: Manchester University Press, 1992), 142–3.

18 Keith Thomas, 'Commentary', *Times Literary Supplement*, 7 May 2010.

19 Roger Smith, *Being Human: Historical Knowledge and the Creation of Human Nature* (Manchester: Manchester University Press, 2007), 258, with his italics.

20 Brian Vickers (ed.), *Francis Bacon: A Critical Edition of the Major Works* (Oxford: Oxford University Press, 1996), 205. For a stimulating more recent argument, see Jared Diamond 'Epilogue: The Future of Human History as Science' in Jared Diamond, *Guns, Germs and Steel: A Short History of Everybody for the Last 13,000 Years* (London: Vintage, 2005).

21 See, for example, 'Climate Change & the UN Copenhagen Summit', *Royal Society of Edinburgh Briefing Paper (09–05)*, December 2009. And see also the Intergovernmental Panel on Climate Control's *IPCC News* 1, January 2010, for a response to criticisms of the Fourth Assessment Report. Online: http://www.ipcc.ch/pdf/Newsletter/IPCC_newsletter_2010_issue_1.pdf (accessed 3 March 2011).

22 See, for example, 'Computing for the future of the planet', *Philosophical Transactions of the Royal Society*, Series A, October 2008.

23 See also Peter Middleton, 'How Novels Can Contribute to our Understanding of Climate Change', in Levene and others, *History at the End of the World?*.

24 *Bulletin of the Atomic Scientists* 14 January 2010. Online: http://www.thebulletin. org/content/media-center/announcements/2010/01/14/it-6-minutes-to-midnight (accessed 3 March 2011).

25 E. V. Tarle, 'Ocherednaia zadacha', *Annaly: zhurnal vseobshchei istorii* 1(1921): 17–18.

26 See, for example, chapters 1–4 in Levene and others, *History at the End of the World?*.

27 McNeill, *Something New*, 362. See also 'The Anthropocene: a new epoch of geological time?', *Philosophical Transactions of the Royal Society*, Series A, March 2011. For a perspicacious essay by Dipesh Chakrabarty, 'The Climate of History: Four Theses', see online: http://www.sciy.org/2009/12/23/ (accessed 25 March 2011).

INDEX

Lightning Source UK Ltd.
Milton Keynes UK

176036UK00002B/1/P